BUILDING THE WORD

BUILDING THE WORD

The Dynamics of Communication and Preaching

J. Randall Nichols

HARPER & ROW, PUBLISHERS

SAN FRANCISCO

Cambridge   London
Hagerstown   Mexico City
Philadelphia   São Paulo
New York 1817 Sydney

FIRST EDITION

Designed by Jim Mennick

Library of Congress Cataloging in Publication Data

Nichols, J. Randall.
  BUILDING THE WORD.

  Includes bibliographical references and index.
  1. Preaching. I. Title.
BV4211.2.N48 1980   251   79-3590
ISBN 0-06-066109-7

80 81 82 83 84 10 9 8 7 6 5 4 3 2 1

To the memories of Paul Scherer and Royal C. Nemiah,
who kept the word alive and who, should they chance to meet,
will enjoy each other's company

Contents

Preface   ix

I. WHY BUILD AT ALL?
   THE PURPOSES OF PREACHING REVISITED   1

   Chapter 1.   The Perils of Explanation   2
   Chapter 2.   Healing Is the Point   7
   Chapter 3.   Conviction Is What You Hope to
                  Beat   12
   Chapter 4.   A Warning Before
                  Groundbreaking   17

II. THE BASIC DESIGN
    STRATEGIES FOR PREPARATION AND PREACHING . .   25

    Chapter 5.   An Eisegesis Revival   26
    Chapter 6.   Over- and Underpreparation . . .   30
    Chapter 7.   Overworked Concreteness   35
    Chapter 8.   Preaching for Yourself   39
    Chapter 9.   Relevance May Be Irrelevant . . .   44

III. SPECS AND MATERIALS
     THE TACTICS OF PREACHING   51

     Chapter 10. The Magic Number 7   52
     Chapter 11. The Languages of Preaching.
                    I: The Jerusalem Connection . .   58

Chapter 12. The Languages of Preaching.
             II: The Unfolding Context   . . .   69
Chapter 13. Diagnosis: The Missing Step   . . .   75

IV. LIVING IN THE BLUEPRINT
     THE RECEIVING END OF PREACHING   89

Chapter 14. Sharing the Study   90
Chapter 15. The Work of the Kitchen:
             Digestion   94
Chapter 16. Guided Tours, or How to Listen
             to a Sermon   98
Chapter 17. Company Coming   106

V.   BACK TO THE DRAWING BOARD
     METHODS THAT WORK   115

Chapter 18. Power Planning   116
Chapter 19. The Idea Inventory   135
Chapter 20. Getting to Know the Clients:
             Case Studies and Preaching   . . .   140
Chapter 21. Preserving Historic Sites:
             Embarrassment Becoming
             Opportunity   144
Chapter 22. Consumer Protection:
             A Bill of Rights for
             Congregations   158

Notes   163
Index   169

Preface

For reasons I will never know, I discovered one day that I had stopped talking about "writing" sermons, or "creating" them, or "preparing" them. I was talking, instead, about "building" them. Where the image came from is a mystery; but once I realized I had it, or that it had me, we grew to be friends and have done each other favors on several occasions. I hope this is one of them.

To think of a sermon being "built" instead of being "written" sounds about right for expressing both the creativity and the utility that preaching calls forth from its practitioners. People use these things we build to live in or work in or get well in. Sometimes we build better than we know, and sometimes we violate every zoning ordinance in the book. What draws us together, all of us who preach, is the central conviction that unless the Lord builds these houses we call "sermons" they will surely be in vain. Whatever else we may say, nothing can top that, ever. Meanwhile, we have some work to do.

In the first part of my career as a teacher of preaching, I heeded the great theories of proclamation and communication and frightened my students. In the second stage of my career, I listened to proponents of the wisdom of homiletics writing and bored my students. In the third phase of my career, I listened to the consumers of my own preaching and flattered myself undeservedly. Now, in the fourth part of my teaching career, I am listening to people who do not always think they are talking about preaching—therapists, theologians, teachers, and novelists—and have begun, in some small measure, to intrigue my students.

My motivation is, I hope, honest and simple: somewhere along the line it dawned on me that most of what I knew or taught that was helpful about preaching had come not so much from the great and small writings on the subject as it had from *reacting to* those writings, sometimes in a plainly argumentative way. What I found myself teaching to seminary students was not often found in print, except insofar as I argued with the "conventional wisdom" about preaching, sometimes with a fair amount of heat. I became a sort of rebel, so far as traditional homiletics goes, although I hope not a mean-tempered one.

I want to contribute to what working preachers understand and practice in their own pulpit work. I sometimes call these paragraphs heresies simply because the weight of traditional writing and talking in homiletics is against them. I have no wish to be cute or combative. I *do* wish to turn some of our common assumptions upside down and see whether a fresh perspective on the truth might be found there. No one, surely, will agree with everything I have to say. But if someone finds the gleaming edge of a new insight on his or her preaching poking out between these pages, and then if some pew sitter down the line finds the truth of life in Jesus Christ canted at a slightly more accessible angle than it was before, then my purpose has been met.

A word about the readers I have in mind. I am thinking most of all of preachers, whether they are beginning a career, re-thinking one, waging one, or ending one. I am not trying to make an airtight theoretical case (although I would like to think it could be done for each of the points of this volume) so much as I am wanting to talk to preaching students and practitioners about next Sunday. If the audience could be live now, I would envision it as an informal continuing education seminar for preachers of all kinds, with you and me talking back and forth about our common task, acknowledging that we each have something to contribute but that for a little while at least I am going to do most of the talking. Some of what I say is going to be new, some of it is going to be strange, and some of it (God willing) will be useful in ways you cannot quite put your finger on just yet. Let us begin.

1

WHY BUILD AT ALL?
The Purposes of Preaching
Revisited

It is almost *de rigueur* to begin a book on preaching by questioning and talking about its overall aim and purpose. With so many different books doing that, you would think we would have made up our minds by now. Not so, however, and probably a good thing. Preaching is a highly complex and multivalent activity, no matter how stylized it may become in this or that traditional way. Any preacher who stops to think about it can probably find a half dozen different purposes for his or her pulpit work, all of them appropriate to different preaching contexts, clienteles, or moments in history.

Our purpose here is not so much to add to the list as it is to turn some of its most common assumptions upside-down to see some things we may have missed. There is a lot more that could be said, to be sure. What we want to do now is stop at three commonly held views of the purpose of preaching and needle each of them a bit in the interest of shedding some fresh light on preaching's inner communicative dynamics.

It is not as easy a task as it sounds. Clement Welsh, who as Warden of the College of Preachers in Washington, D.C., works with hundreds of Episcopal preachers, commented recently that the hardest thing for his continuing education clients to do is answer the question "What do you hope to accomplish in a sermon?" My own experience with seminary students and ministers in continuing education settings bears that observation out. It also has found that when preachers finally do succeed in answering the question of purpose, four ingredients are likely to appear in some variation or other in what they say: (1) *explanation* of the Bible, theological topics, the hearers themselves, or the world we live and try to be faithful in; (2) *helping people feel better* about themselves, their situations, and their neighbors; (3) building a sense of *conviction* of our sinfulness, in service to our readiness to repent and be saved; and (4) *love* as the source of Christian energy for the whole business.

It is to those four oft-listed ingredients of purpose that we now turn.

Chapter 1. **The Perils of Explanation**

Let us begin with a blunt heretical suggestion: the purpose of preaching is not to explain anything, not even the Bible. The purpose of preaching is to extend an invitation. Child psychologist Fitzhugh Dodson's advice to parents serves equally well for preachers: "Thou shalt not talk excessively to a child." He reports a conversation overheard between playmates at nursery school, culminating in one child's threat to the other: "I'll hit you! I'll cut you up in little pieces! I'll—I'll—I'll *explain* it to you!"[1]

Now it may be true, as some have said, that the average members of a congregation are largely illiterate about their Bible, their theological heritage, and the religious issues of the day. And it may even be true that it would on the whole be good for them to know more than they do about those things. Our mistake lies in therefore assuming that in preaching explanation—of text, theology, or religion—is what is called for. In the first place, no one will absorb any information he or she does not in some felt way have a need to absorb. Harry Emerson Fosdick said it best in his famous quip that people do not usually come to church with a burning desire to learn whatever happened to the Jebusites.[2] In the second place, if a person's need to know something is high enough for explanation to work at all, it probably will not take much outside prodding or guiding. One does not, by and large, need to explain the menu to a hungry person.

We preachers are at our worst in the explanation department when we use perfectly good stories or illustrations in sermons but then explain them to death right afterward. Time and again what might have been an inviting, creatively ambiguous narrative where a listener could dwell for a time to learn and grow does not survive the preacher's next lines, which begin with "Now let us see what this means for us. . . ." The very idea of "illustration" in homiletics could use an overhaul. In one sense, an "illustration" suggests a drawing to explain, make more understandable, or render applicable something in some other form—words or objects or ideas. In our technological society, we are accustomed to thinking of illustrations as explainers of what might otherwise be unclear. All parents who have spent Christmas Eve assembling their children's gifts—especially the ones labeled "Easy assembly, no tools required"—know the value of an illustration for explanatory purposes. Explaining the illustration that was supposed to explain something else is a little on the absurd side.

But there is another use for illustration, and it is a shame that this one has taken second place in preaching: *illustrations can be used to invite a person into a realm of experience.* One paradigm for this use of illustrations is none other than the books that parents read to their children night after night. In the best ones, the illustrations explain nothing, add no new information, make nothing clearer than the words already did. No, what they do is open the door for a brief visual visit to another world where dwell Reddy Fox and the Little Prince and the Pokey Puppy and the Velvetine Rabbit and the Hardy Boys and Super-Heroes old and new. Invitation, not explanation, is the purpose of preaching and the work of its "illustrations."

The difference between explanation and invitation is as much a matter of approach and the "posture" of the preacher as anything. Perhaps it was a reaction to the excesses of exhortation and revivalism, or perhaps it was faith in education, gone wild; whatever the reason, a lot of preaching has succumbed to the subtle assumption that if only we are clear enough in explaining the meaning of a passage of the Bible, or a topic of social action, or a "proposition" that lies at the base of a sermon, then the work has been done. To think of preaching as invitation requires a different posture altogether. For one thing, an invitation is *to* something (which we will talk about in the next chapter), and the response you look for is not agreement or disagreement, understanding or confusion, truth or falsehood, even liking or disliking, so much as it is whether people come to the party or not. For another thing, an invitation is by its nature incomplete and one-sided as it stands, and preachers need to be reminded that if they are preaching well their sermons are seldom ever complete in and of themselves. Like invitations, they start a process, they do not finish it. Explanations, by contrast, when they are finished are just that: over and done with. Few of us really want to think of preaching that way any more.

Theologically speaking, the recent surge of interest in story, narrative, and experience as basic theological forms ought to translate, homiletically, into a renewed emphasis on invitation rather than explanation. That is what the function of a story *is*. A listener yearns to be addressed by transcendence, not informed about God; and if a listener does not yearn for anything, matters are even more basic. The need for invitation, even if it must be to a consciousness of pain and lack, is paramount.

Ah, but you may say, this is a word trick, a way to sugar-coat the pill. In the end, we really want people to *know*, do we not? And who can blame us for fudging just a little on dictionary meanings to make life easier? Not so. In an age of information overload, what we want in preaching, as Clement Welsh pointed out, is not more information about anything, but a chance to put things together so life has meaning.[3] A personal recollection: once I was a guest preacher in a smallish congregation, and my sermon was on Ezekiel 37, the Valley of Dry Bones. I was going on with some vigor about spirit and breath and life when two elderly ladies in the back rose from their pew and briskly but quietly left. Good heavens, I thought, surely no one could take offense at this stuff, and on the other hand people who are plainly bored have long since learned to suffer in silent inactivity until the benediction (when, as John Fry once said, the captives get set free[4]). What was going on? All became clear at the end of the service, when the two intrepid ladies appeared once again at the church door where I was shaking hands. They apologized for leaving, explaining that they lived together and that during my sermon, for some reason they could not quite figure out, it suddenly hit them that they could not remember whether they had turned off the gas stove before coming to church! (I'm not going to explain that. Would you?)

One of the things going on when preachers succumb to explanation as a preaching goal has to do with our uneasiness about uncertainty. Learning theorists have long been saying that the most effective learning goes on in the presence of optimal uncertainty—the tug of dissatisfaction that leads us into wanting to know more.[5] Novelty, inconsistency, conflict, and uncertainty are all terms pointing to the same central dynamic, our built-in human need to bring things into completion and focus, which is activated to begin with by the sense of *in*completion and *lack* of focus.[6] We know both from common sense and from empirical investigation that either too much or too little uncertainty works against the learning and discovery process—hence the crucial word *optimal* when talking about it.[7] Too little "pull," and we never overcome the mental inertia of being satisfied with where we are; too much, and we are swamped with hopeless confusion.

All well and good; but what happens when that perspective on learning bumps into the theological values of faith and conviction that we are taught to believe lie at the heart of proclamation? It is surely not the uncertain trumpet that announces the good news; if anything, we sense these days a need for boldness in preaching, for a recovery of that sense of pastoral authority that can support and lead people from the pulpit.

The more you probe it, the more that looks like a real parting of the ways between the theological and the psychological understanding of human communication. Part of the appeal of evangelicalism lies in its seeming recovery of certainty and purpose, especially in preaching. We are stuck with a real dilemma, something like "How do we sing the Lord's song of sure salvation in the foreign land of our ignorance and incompleteness?" If those are the conditions under which we work, how indeed can preaching take place? If it takes some kind of uncertainty for human learning, discovery, and communication to occur, how then do we proclaim the gospel rather than scratch our heads in public about it?

Not so strangely, almost exactly that unanswered—and perhaps unanswerable—question was the foundation of Karl Barth's theological work.[8] How indeed is it possible for preachers to speak about God? We are standing at the shoreline of a mystery—a *crisis* in Barthian terms. It will not go away; it will not be decided. God remains God, wholly other, unspeakable, transcendent; humankind remains what it is, reaching for but never grasping God, as far from being able to speak of God as from being able to portray the flight of a bird. And here, suddenly, is the unexpected answer: the certainty we preach is not after all the sureness of having arrived at the Kingdom, on the other side of the gap between human and divine. It is not anything that could be explained. No, the certainty we preach is that God invites us precisely into the crisis of the universe with its unceasing tension and dialectic *and that we are not destroyed.* The discovery of the grace of Jesus Christ is hearing the voice in the whirlwind; our uncertainty is our acknowledgment and our witness of the incarnation: against overwhelming odds, we are not destroyed.

Ulrich Simon has said that a theology of crisis is only worthy of the name when it invites our participation in the crisis, most probably when we would really like a little rest.[9] The ceaseless dialectic of question and answer, humankind and God, yes and no, turns out to be, to our amazement, not only the process of communication but also the content of proclamation. Our work as preachers ceases to be explanation; it becomes invitation to that process, and the only certainty we have is that it is the domain of the waiting, unreachable, transcendent God who is *for us.* That is enough.

Chapter 2. **Healing Is the Point**

Some of the most satisfying times in a pastor's life are when the investment, even the agony, of ministry makes people feel better than they did before. The heart and soul of a pastor is somewhere near the idea of leaving the universe and its inhabitants fractionally better off than they were a little while—say, a lifetime—ago. Therein lies an occupational hazard for preaching not often talked about: it is awfully easy to settle for making people feel good when what is needed is healing.

Healing means a lot of things, although let us be clear that in these pages it does not mean walking the sawdust trail, speaking in tongues, televised laying on of hands, or any of the assorted guruisms that plague us. To a preacher, healing means at least four things: clarity, freedom, illumination, and reality. Innocent sounding as they are, the surprising thing is that we have so easily accepted substitutes when it comes to preaching.

Take clarity, for instance, the very idea of being able to look life in the face and see what is really there, especially if a mirror is included in the scene. Before we know it, we are talking about something like *simplicity* instead: keeping ideas simple, making theological points simple, simplifying our prose, heading for a simple faith. The trouble is, lots of things we have to deal with are not simple. There is nothing simple about trying to find God's will for one's life when it gets down to brass tacks. There is nothing simple about telling a four-year-old his daddy just died. Simplicity is not known to characterize the inner workings of, let us say, a local church women's association or an all-male board of deacons. A minister in therapy remembered her preacher father haranguing his congregation and family about "making it through to heaven" while her mother wept for fear her only child would be "lost" even as that child sat bewildered in the pew. That was simple, all right; it was also sick.

Clarity is something else. People who find themselves caught in the tangles of life are not suffering from complexity so much as befuddlement and the loss of meaning. The healing that we invite people to in Christ's name through our preaching does not settle for simplicity; it aims for clarity, for helping people see more clearly than they did before who they are, what God has to do with them, what loving their neighbors amounts to, most particularly when things are *not* simple. As I look back on student sermon manuscripts, I recall few if any that suffered either in their conceptualization or their prose style by anything that simplifying could cure; it is the opacity that will not let us see through to the ends of things that causes trouble. It is far better that a preacher aim for clarity both as a goal and as a criterion of preaching than to go through the often amazing mental gymnastics called for to make life simple in the face of insuperable odds.

Few would argue that freedom is a second element of the healing to which preaching invites us. However, when we let ourselves wonder whether we sometimes confuse freedom with *easiness*, the plot thickens. If anything, freedom in these days of multiple and conflicting loyalties is going to be tough. The Christian perspective has always thought of freedom in tandem with commitment, not with getting away from (or with) something. We tend to lose that distinction in preaching and to settle for comfort instead. I cannot offhand remember hearing a sermon in which the preacher confessed that anything was going to be *hard*—from understanding a parable to living with a teenager. Charlie Rich has more hold of the theological question in his song "Nothing in the World (to Do with Me)," in the line, "I'd like to call her just to ask her how it feels to be free."

To be sure, freedom and ease are not polar opposites, one ruling the other out. The point is that preaching has to wrestle with the temptation to want to make things easier for people, when its theological commitment to healing calls for freeing the captives—who just may not find being free particularly easy after all. One of the most haunting personal confessions ever written was Viktor Frankl's reflection on being freed from a Nazi death camp:

> In the evening [after being liberated] when we all met again in our hut, one said secretly to the other, "Tell me, were you pleased today?" And the other replied, feeling ashamed as he did not know that we all felt similarly, "Truthfully, no." We had literally lost the ability to feel pleased and had to relearn it slowly.[1]

Illumination is a third factor of healing. A semantic battle over the differences between clarity and illumination would be pointless. The idea for preaching is that, if clarity means being able to see clear through to the ends of things, illumination is the dawning sense of hope and the meaning of those things to what and who and where one clearly is. Clarity is what Oedipus achieves in Sophocles' *Oedipus the King*, leading to his ironic blindness; illumination does not come until *Oedipus at Colonnus*, when the tragic hero is taken to the gods. Illumination is that

sense of congruence and significance for which preachers all
too easily substitute *happiness.* Here is the rub: happiness cannot
do double duty for illumination. "Don't tell me, I don't want to
know" is a formula for some kind of happiness, but it leaves its
holder blind as a bat. There ought to be at least a beatitude
against it. One of the most supportive aphorisms I ever heard
was simply this: no one is happy all of the time.

Getting a sense of perspective on life, finding the shadowy
corners lighted up and the scare gone, having my worst suspi-
cions confirmed about who loves me and who does not are all
part of the healing that illumination brings. No one ever said
it would be a romp through pure happiness. Some few dare to
breathe that there might be times with little happiness at all.
Christian faith puts its confidence in the light that was the light
of the world, knowing very good and well what it cost. Preaching
invites people to that.

Abram Kardiner, a psychoanalyst, once said with profound
simplicity, "The only cure for neurosis is reality." The fourth
thing healing means is being in touch with reality more than
with its cuckoolike displacement in the pulpit, *organization.* It is
not as implausible a choice as one might first think. A great deal
of preaching inadvertently puts more emphasis on getting
things organized than on getting them in touch with reality,
particularly things of the mind like beliefs or values or theological assumptions. When we plunge into the subject of a sermon,
it is somehow crucially important to get all the loose ends tied
up before the benediction, whether they are so neatly arranged
in reality or not. Find the next 100 sermons at random on why
God lets children die or how come the church is such a fractious
gang of adolescents, and you will with a certainty find a large
number of them fundamentally concerned with getting
thoughts and experiences *organized* so there are a minimum
number of paradoxes, unanswered questions, unsoothed hurts,
and unincluded middles. It does not always matter what the
words at the end are. The very form of the sermon, if not the
music of the preacher's voice, will leave us comfortably seduced

into thinking that whatever the answer was it was at least *an answer*. For every sermon that helps its listeners confront and deal realistically with their anger, mistrust, and manipulativeness toward one another and toward God, there must be at least a dozen others that assure us of the all-rightness of things once we get organized into the right kind of koinonia, action group, or theological chorale.

The fact is, though, Christian faith affirms that the healing presence of its Lord has a way of coming into the *dis*order of life, with no promises that the machinery will ever run any better. What it promises is that God never was confined to the proper order of things in spirit, body, or community, and that real creation came out of real chaos, and still does. I have never read a better demonstration of the difference than William Muehl's story of the broken gift. Here it is.

> One December afternoon many years ago a group of parents stood in the lobby of a nursery school waiting to claim their children after the last pre-Christmas class session. As the youngsters ran from their lockers, each one carried in his hands the "surprise," the brightly wrapped package on which he had been working diligently for weeks. One small boy, trying to run, put on his coat, and wave, all at the same time, slipped and fell. The "surprise" flew out of his grasp, landed on the tile floor, and broke with an obvious ceramic crash.
>
> The child's first reaction was one of stunned silence. But in a moment he set up an inconsolable wail. His father, thinking to comfort him, knelt down and murmured, "Now it doesn't matter, son. It doesn't really matter."
>
> But his mother, much wiser in such affairs, swept the boy into her arms and said, "Oh, but it does matter. It matters a great deal." And she wept with her son.

Any preacher who has ever in his or her sermon committed the equivalent atrocity at a theological level of telling a kid with a bloody knee from the gravel driveway that it doesn't hurt needs to bump into reality once again. Christ's healing is there and nowhere else. It *does* matter.

Settling for comfort rather than healing is probably as much accidental as intentional among preachers. Few would gainsay the appropriateness of clarity, freedom, illumination, and reality as constituent parts of the healing preaching invites us to. No one would actually espouse their logical opposites—perhaps confusion, bondage, darkness, and fantasy. The danger comes from a more subtle point of view on preaching that holds something like simplicity, easiness, happiness, or organization as cardinal virtues both for the preacher's style as well as the preacher's goal with people. The point here is not only that those are not primary allegiances but, moreover, that there may be times when healing means setting them aside for the sake of something more life giving. Healing is to be found by entering into the "crisis continuum of the universe" as Simon says, not by avoiding it.[3] If we are inviting people to something, they ought to know what it is, really.

Chapter 3. **Conviction Is What You Hope to Beat**

The old phrase "preaching for conviction" (or still worse, "preaching for *a* conviction") is seldom heard these days, but the idea is far from dead. The intended meaning was not, by the way, preaching to try to help people have more conviction or earnestness about their faith. No, what it meant was conviction in the forensic sense of being convicted for a misdeed—being human, for example. The idea was that if you could get people to own up to their badness then they would be more inclined to do whatever was needed to get saved. What "badness" or "saved" meant was adaptable to a variety of situations and prejudices. In modern times, for instance, you might find a preacher happily saying that if people could only get in touch with and put down the "Parent" part of their psyches (in Transactional Analysis terms) then they would be able to free their "Creative Child" for heaven knows what kind of fulfillment. The vernacular has changed, not the conviction formula.

It is surprising to find with both lay and clergy groups that even the old language is still stoutly defended in some quarters. Just below the surface of even some of the best of our preaching is a veiled sadism that believes getting people to feel bad about something is at least half if not all of the preacher's work. I have heard sermons from capable seminary students that were nothing short of verbal abuse, and what made them hard to criticize was knowing that too many preachers and congregations thought that was the way it ought to be.

Healing, however, leads not to "conviction" but to something else—perhaps "commissioning" is as good a term today as when Barth first used it to describe preaching's purpose.[1] You almost never find Jesus calling for repentance alone; commissioning to a task in his name invariably follows. Somewhere we lost touch with that. Christian response came to be individualized, privatized, and psychologized, in roughly that order. Privatization has become one of the most dangerous but pervasive trends in social consciousness today. Krister Stendahl once addressed the American Psychological Association, of all people, with the message that the writings of Paul look very different when you take away the psychologization that modern Western thought has put on them.[2] Individualization, privatization, and psychologization of the gospel are the handmaidens of preaching for conviction. A listener stands convicted—and stands alone; the verdict is an inner one—between you and your God; the response is subjective—you feel guilty, and maybe your attitude changes. The longer we stay with the language of conviction, the farther it seems from "Feed my sheep" or "Go into all nations" or Karl Barth's unwavering insistence on our "divine commission" to proclaim the gospel.

Preaching for commission, by contrast, has a considerably different angle to it. It is defined by two points. The first is an uncomfortable certainty that we human beings will never be fully ready for our work as disciples, simply because we will never stop being fully human with all the sinfulness that entails. The work of Christ is not something you do after you repent, because you can never repent enough to get started if that is what it takes. But the second point keeps that first one from becoming the depressing end of all responsibility: discipleship this side of the eschaton is a *process* of faithfulness rather than an *outcome* of faith. If the process will never be finished (and it will not), then we may in the meantime be strengthened by knowing that it does not have to be finished in order for us to be claimed and loved by God (and it does not). Preaching for commission has a way of getting around the barrier of our masochism and under the collapse of our self-esteem. It says that, no matter how damning the evidence, we still count for something in the universe, and we have something to give not because we have contrived it but simply because God did not make us otherwise. The worship of the commissioned has to do with bringing an offering to God and his creation; that of the convicted strives for getting a blessing on the botch we have made of things. Preaching both reflects and reinforces the difference, often in ways it does not fully realize.

The idea of commissioning as a goal for preaching is, of course, a very active one; the word itself suggests doing something or failing that at least being poised for the doing given the opportunity. If we followed tradition, we would now begin to talk of Christian love either as the motive power of Christian doing or as the outcome of our commissioning. So speaking, we would be in lots of distinguished company, but we would also be wrong. Being commissioned to love sounds good for a while—until you begin to wonder what love is *not*, if it is so pervasive as to be something one is commissioned for. In a word, the idea of love may not carry all the weight we have wanted it to, especially if we begin to peek out from behind our privatism into the world of relationships and systems and forces to which preaching commissions us.[3] Paul Scherer used to quote Don Marquis affectionately in saying, "If you stroke a cliché long enough pretty soon it will begin to purr like an epigram."[4] Is the reverse true too? Does love begin to lose its savor with overuse? Some would say so.

Seward Hiltner has an ingenious way of poking through even the most respectable social and theological shibboleths, as, for instance, when talking about medicine and health in our society he asks, "By the way, just how much health is enough?"[5] Ouch. We are not supposed to talk about "health"—of which one cannot possibly have too much, can one?—that way.

The same hands-off policy has long applied to love in the Christian vocabulary, although James Barr, for one, has at least tried to clear away some of the romantic fog around the terms *agape* and *eros*.[6] It is surely safe to guess that hardly ever has the Protestant pulpit seriously asked "How much love is enough, anyway?" And rarer still, one imagines, is the sermon that suggests that *aggression* might be a good thing—a Christian virtue, in fact, and sometimes to be preferred over love. Precisely such a suggestion is the burden of this chapter.

Hiltner reminds us that the word *aggression* has come to have negative and disruptive connotations only fairly recently as these things go.[7] Initially, as a Latin term, *adgressus*, it meant simply "progressing toward a goal." "Aggressiveness," which these days we would almost universally associate with such negative things as attack, bad manners, and threat, potentially means the capacity *to move toward a goal with deliberation and purpose.* Occasionally even popular usage lets a little positive flavor creep in. We sometimes speak favorably, for instance, of someone aggressively pursuing something or other, or we may praise a formerly passive and retiring person's growing capacity to be aggressive. Often, of course, we cover our bets by using the phrase "appropriately aggressive," or by saying something like "aggressive, in the positive sense."

Now how does all that get related to love? There is no logical

connection, no etymological kinship, no implication that one is
the opposite of the other. Hiltner's suggestion is simply that we
have tried to make the concept of love cover too many bases,
whereas in some cases aggression rightly understood is what
we really have wanted to say all along. The differentiation he
proposes, and it is a good one for preachers to keep in mind,
is that *love* tends to apply to the cultivation of relationships,
while *aggression* ought to be used to speak of moving toward a
goal. Love is more self-oriented, either one's own or another's,
and aggression is more purpose oriented. The trouble with
confusing the two ideas is that *love* when overused becomes
squishy, romantic, and pious, while *aggression* becomes nasty,
hyperactive, and frightening. The heresy we propose here is
that a lot of preaching talks about living the Christian life with
love when it really ought to be aiming toward living the Christian life with aggression. When you want to plant a tree, you use
a shovel; when you harvest its fruit, you get a basket. The two
cannot be interchanged. Preachers have been trying to make
love baskets into shovels and other tools for generations. Why
not try something better suited for the task?

It might come as a great relief for people to hear their
preacher interpret aggression that way, and to say that this too
is what we bring to our work as commissioned Christian people.
It would certainly save us the logical embarrassment and the
emotional phoniness of trying to reduce everything somehow
to a relationship matter under the rubric of love. Some things
just do not fit: voting your oil company proxies to confront
South African apartheid, raising your voice to question whether
nuclear power is really progress, taking sides with the earth and
its needs against the bulldozers and developers, driving a truck
to deliver hot meals to senile old people who forget to cook, or
finishing off the church's unused basement to house a class for
autistic children. There are lots of things, concrete and abstract, activist and attitudinal, sacred and secular, to which we
are commissioned in Christ's name that just are not covered by
"love" in any direct and identifiable sense. Trying to shoehorn

everything into love only feeds our already keen tendency to privatize, individualize, and psychologize our motives, actions, and responsibilities. No, let us have aggression—making progress toward a goal—with the mind of Christ. And let us be theologically clear than when we lack aggression—Christian aggression, if you must—no matter how loving we feel we are just plain falling down on the job. One suspects that an awful lot of angry sermons have been preached counterproductively on love just because their authors knew something was fishy about that, but did not have any alternative. No more.

Chapter 4. **A Warning Before Groundbreaking**

Most of us do not like to talk or write about negative aspects of preaching, and that aversion has led to a very serious neglect. Most of us believe that the worst outcome of preaching is some kind of neutral ineffectiveness; we have little sense of the actual harm we can do. I have never read a line in any homiletics book or article that even remotely hinted that preaching done badly can by any more harmful than your everyday waste of time. The point here is simple: *we should be less worried about boring people and more concerned for not harming them.* Medicine's ethical foundation is the famous "Do no harm," as complicated a dictum though that may be in modern health care. Preaching's motto too often has seemed to be "Don't be a bore."

We preachers have succumbed, it would seem, to a kind of sacralized narcissism, through which we worry obsessively about being interesting, relevant, understandable, and the rest, all of which have more to do with how we appear in the eyes of our consumers than with how they fare in their attempts to live lives of faith and responsibility, often against insuperable odds. There are, for instance, very few writings especially in theological or pastoral circles on the subject of religious pathology, yet every psychotherapist encounters client after client part of whose suffering and dysfunction is immediately connected with some aspect of religious belief, practice, or experience that likely as not was presided over by preaching.

It would be bad enough if we stopped at being narcissistic but harmless. Unfortunately, there is more to be said. From a communication analysis point of view, the preacher with a more or less consistent group of listeners on a regular basis over a period of time is in one of the most powerful positions imaginable for influencing, for good or ill, the values, beliefs, patterns of relationship and interactions of his or her people. The preacher, for instance, who week in and week out subtly adopts magical solutions for real problems is cultivating a similar pattern of belief and value among those who trust what they hear. When we preach out of an unhealthy dependency on external forces at the expense of our own responsibilities, we invite our people to do the same. Whether the underlying idea of God in our sermons is that of wrathful father, manipulative autocrat, impotent has-been, or otherworldly dreamer, it goes into the mix of what our listeners bring to their responses to life and death. In short, when we think of the communicative "work" of preaching as having to do with cultivating people's developing images of reality, right and wrong, relationship, and importance, then it should be clear that preaching is a potent force that cannot be thought of as merely benign at its worst.[1]

The preaching that constantly intellectualizes, no matter how cleverly or understandably, cultivates in its consumers a view of reality that has little room for the life of the spirit or the whole range of human feelings. The preaching that admonishes its people in one form or another never to give themselves credit for anything true or noble or to respect the possibilities of their motives also teaches a chronic distrust of human beings. When preaching ever so implicitly suggests, week after week, that human beings are helpless in the face either of implacably malignant fate *or* of amazing grace, it also nurtures the spirit of helplessness that lies behind depression and psychosomatic illness.[2] When the preacher in thousands of pulpits over thousands of Sunday mornings more than hints that the dead are somehow not really dead and gone—whatever else we say after that—it should not surprise us that dealing with separation, death, and grief is one of the things our people have most trouble with these days. And no such list as this should be left without mention of the week in and week out judgment that "we" have somehow caused the world's starvation, enslavement, and inhumanity and ought to do something in recompense, which inevitably leads to a part of our frustration, guilt, and impotence on both personal and national levels.

The list could go on, but harangue is not the purpose. What I am trying to plant is the idea that preaching is a potent force in the development of the human beings who receive it regularly, and our strong commitment to its life-giving and transcendence-mediating power ought to be balanced by a healthy respect for its capacity to harm. One generalization that can be made about medications is that the most dramatically life-giving ones are also the most poisonous when wrongly used. Not even vitamins and aspirin are exempt. Neither should preaching be.

The danger of a "Don't be a bore" ethic for preaching becomes apparent only when one takes seriously the communicative power of preaching *apart from* the actual informational content of any one sermon. That is to say, in any message, including preaching, there are at least two levels of result to be considered. One is the obvious content of a message: the factual information, the opinions, the value judgments, the exhortations, the questions that make up the semantic level of any message and about which most writing about preaching spends most of its time.

There is a second level that is not so obvious. If the first could be called "semantic," the second might be named "valuational." Think of it analogously to the unconscious part of our mental lives. We seldom perceive it directly, but it influences the very *way* we deal with other things, including the information of messages. At this second level, we pay attention to such things as the frequency of a particular subject or a kind of illustration in sermon after sermon, leading implicitly but steadily to a judgment of how real and how important it must be; the way uncertainty, paradox, or question is handled in sermon after sermon, leading to some automatic assumptions about how we should deal with those things in daily living; the appearance of "success stories" in sermons, leading us to some opinions, often painful, about how we live out failures and setbacks as God's people.

Included here is the list of horrors of a few paragraphs earlier —these and more are second-level features of messages that without a deliberate act of reflection we preachers will for the most part not be aware of, any more than most people are aware of the underlying values and principles of their day in and day out actions. The danger is that we tend too easily to become thoroughly gnostic in our preaching, assuming that only the manifest content is of importance. Surely one contribution the whole pastoral care and counseling movement has made, though, is to alert us to the telling importance of what is not so immediately obvious to such inspection as hearing the words of a sermon. Harry Emerson Fosdick was only the first of many to report that when his sermons dealt directly with the pastoral needs and concerns of someone he had in mind, the number of people who came to him for pastoral care in the following week increased dramatically. That is not so much a guarantee of counseling business as it is a tip-off of the work of preaching and how important it can be—both for good and for ill.

Now that does not mean we should suddenly become preoccupied with the potential hazards of our preaching, past, present, and future, in the manner of health food faddists who see carcinogens behind every pleasure known to humankind.

Nor does it mean that we either can or should subject each and every utterance to meticulous inspection for its covert significance, as in the famous cartoon of one psychiatrist saying to another, "Good morning" and in the next frame the other wondering, "What did he mean by that?" But all this surely *does* mean that we adopt a considerably more humble and more realistic attitude toward preaching—less narcissistic and less defensive; more respectful and more confident. It surely means that we take a long look at our working assumptions both theologically and experientially, taking it as a certainty that some way or other they will be expressed in our preaching. One of the most penetrating but most valuable things we can ask ourselves about a sermon is something like this: If people really heard, really believed, and really acted out what we are telling them in sermons, *at all levels,* what would they then be like? Do we want to take responsibility for what we are asking them to get themselves into?

A colleague once confessed that he had thrown away all the sermon manuscripts from his first years of preaching, because, as he read them from the vantage point of more experience and greater knowledge of himself, he was appalled at the anger those sermons contained *that was, not obvious to anyone at the time.* A similar illustration comes from my own experience. People used to preface their visits or phone calls to me, their pastor, with some phrase such as, "I know you're busy and I don't want to take much time. . . ." and I used to respond, humbly and (I thought) supportively, "No, no, that's all right, I've got plenty of time, go ahead." A wise friend who knows far more of such things than I once pointed out the implicit put-down such a reply contained. What it really said was, "I'm not doing anything important, and neither is talking to you." It took a while to break the habit and learn to say, in effect, "Yes, I am busy, but talking to you is important and that is what I want to do."

Sheldon Kopp, in his book *An End to Innocence,* provides a good and almost universal example of the kind of thing at stake here. Kopp, a psychotherapist, writes of that necessarily painful process wherein a child loses its innocent confidence that the world and all its inhabitants can be trusted to fulfill its every wish. We hope the disillusionment will be gradual, tempered by the love and honesty of people close to us. We will grow into a world tainted by inconsistency and threat, but also ripe with creative possibility for love and fulfillment. Sometimes, though, the growing-up process goes awry, and people are overcome by the "raw sense of total vulnerability." They develop "pseudoinnocence" in defense:

> The pseudoinnocent denies his or her own power, identifies self-interest with the design of Providence, and pretends that this is the best of all possible worlds. Such a pose serves to deny feelings of hopelessness, makes the pain of disappointment more bearable, and brings a false sense of order to a chaotic life situation. The cost is high and unforeseen. These same defenses impoverish the possibilities for personal and spiritual growth that unfettered imagination and later life experiences might provide.[3]

Pseudoinnocence—and, even more, its painful collapse when not even such a life-sustaining fiction can be supported—is familiar to every pastor. Without it, we would not even have a theodicy problem in theology. The point here, though, is that preaching can be a tool to help people grow into a realistic sense of trust, responsibility, and the presence of a gracious but not deceptive God; or it can feed the counterfeit confidence of pseudoinnocence with its subtle presumption that suffering is really a good thing, that chaos is a fiction caused by our incomplete knowledge of what God really is up to, that saying the right religious words means all is right with the world no matter what my senses tell me, or with some other easily baptizable distortion of the plain truth. Preaching is a risk. If it were not, it would not be worth doing. Anything that has the power to nurture and shape the formation of something as complex as a human life also has the power to deform it. Our all too common assumptions that the worst preaching can be is boring and that the most havoc it can wreak is disinterest have to be confronted.

When it comes to preaching, are we, too, longing for a lost innocence that frees us from the threat of disappointment at the cost of crippling us for responsibility?

A little later on, we will come to the subject of teaching people how to listen to sermons, and we will be back on this same wavelength. For now, however, suffice it to say that, as a rule, coming clean with your own assumptions, prejudices, incompleteness, and struggle in preaching is at least one road, perhaps the best, to responsibility in preaching. The saying is true and worthy of our homiletical acceptance, that we can handle what is on the table, but what is under it handles us.

II

THE BASIC DESIGN
Strategies for Preparation and Preaching

Before any of us sits down to prepare a sermon, we have already made a number of important decisions, most likely without even being aware of them. Like builders, we have a preference for certain tools to work on certain kinds of materials, and soon their selection becomes automatic. We have a sense of the sequence of events that will eventually lead to a sermon, and at least a rough idea how long the construction is going to take—barring untoward developments in the weather. We know the kind of design we are after, and it is based largely on what we think our clients will accept. With the rising cost of time and materials, we are concerned with function and relevance in our construction. Forty-minute sermons on angelology, like 10-foot ceilings, are not in great demand.

No matter how practiced, however, we would do well from time to time to take stock of what we do automatically. That is the purpose of this section, with its five chapters, one each for five strategic decisions we usually make about tools, construction sequence, style, clientele, and function. In each case, we are going to try a different way of looking at things from the one most of us are used to. The perspectives may be new to you; the work itself is as familiar and basic as last week's sermon preparation.

Chapter 5. An Eisegesis Revival

If anything stands in homiletics as an undoubtedly pure evil, it surely must be eisegesis, the dastardly process of (1) reading into a biblical text whatever it is one wants to find, or, more delicately, (2) of starting sermon preparation with an idea and then finding a text to match. (It is the opposite, of course, of exegesis, which is both orthodox and benign, not to mention unspeakably boring much of the time.) This chapter wants to modify the first horror and flatly challenge the second, both on respectable theological grounds.

As to the first, reading into a text, it is obviously a perversion of biblical exegesis to twist a text out of shape to suit one's own ends—that has never been in doubt. We can wonder, though, whether reading one's own situation and ideas into a text is so bad—or so foreign to what we do anyway with the blessing of biblical scholarship. It can be argued that the meaning of a text only emerges as a reader enters into dialogue with it so that *both* one's original question or point of view *and* what seemed to be the text's external meaning are transformed in what Barth described so vividly as the dialectical encounter of preacher with text. Surely we do not want to say that a text is utterly transparent to its meaning, or that understanding a text should be a mechanical nut-picking process unaffected by the appetite of the preacher.

It is far stronger on theological grounds to say that a text represents a potential opportunity for the Word of God to be heard afresh, that the posture of a preacher is of one being invited into the domain of experience offered by a text, and that what such an invitee brings to that encounter is gathered up, transformed, and reinterpreted *but not ignored* in light of the gospel.

The text represents an opportunity for the Word of God to be heard. A text could be thought of as an interpretative potential, a waiting opportunity for the vitality of the biblical world's original transcendent experience to be rekindled in the present day. Victor Turner suggests, for example, that some archaic symbols of religious import are capable of recreating the original extraordinary experience that gave them birth.[1] Less elegantly, the metaphor of the modern freeze-drying food process suggests how a text might function as a repository of potential experience and significance, which awaits the additive of a hearer-reader's contemporary participation to be reconstituted *in all its original meaning and fullness.* That is the key: the emergent meaning of the text loses nothing of its originality, its claim, or its otherness as it happens in contemporary hermeneutical experience. We need not fear distorting it, so long as we are willing to subject ourselves to its searching dialectic of question and answer. In that process, what I think I bring to a text as my perception of its meaning—as answer, in Barth's terms—is going to be shaken up, turned around, asked to declare itself more fully, and ultimately very likely become more new question than original answer. In short, if I as preacher let the text have its way with what I bring to it, confessing my fundamental "sinfulness" as a reader, so to speak, then I should trust rather than fear for the integrity and vitality of what is there. The Word of God, if we are serious about our capitalization, surely is not so fragile that it will be destroyed by whatever I bring to it.

Obviously, I may be surprised that I come out of a textual experience a different person than I was going in. *That* is what should be said about preaching, rather than a "Do not enter" prohibition against "subjectivity" or a quarantine of a text from the contamination of preunderstanding. Let it be confessed

that there are no guarantees to the process—neither that I will
know exactly what happened, nor that the pristine meaning of
a text will be transparent in my preaching. But to ask for such
guarantees, as we sometimes seem to do when speaking loftily
about the vice of eisegesis, would be to make a claim to perfect-
ability if not perfection of human perception, and we have never
been willing to try for either so long as we have had our theological wits about us.

In fact, the bottom line of this talk about "eisegesis" probably
has to be that there is no power on earth that could stop us from
"reading into" a text no matter how piously we thought we were
preserving its otherness—not, at least, if our understanding of
processes of human perception or communication is even
remotely accurate. One of the basic axioms of communication
theory is that no message is ever "transmitted" with complete
accuracy, like handing a precious cargo over unshaken to its
recipient. Quite the contrary, the communication process is
one of a "receiver's" trying to reconstruct the meaning of a
"message" with as much fidelity to its sender's original intention as possible, but in the sure and certain knowledge that 100
percent accuracy is impossible. The secret of successful communication is not in absolutely accurate decoding of a message,
but rather in being able to allow for and discover the inevitable
errors, changes, and revaluations that are going to occur in the
process—to be able, in other words, to communicate about our
communication.

The same holds for textual interpretation. The assumption
that we will be able to get a text's meaning out whole and
unfingerprinted is silly, if not idolatrous. What preaching
should strive for is the capacity to recognize and take account
of the dialogue we inevitably will have with a text, so that our
conclusions remain both committed and humble before the
transcendent fact of our never being able to "get a leg up on
Jesus," as I once heard it reverentially put. Meaning, in other
words, always bears the machine marks of our own manufacture; what is important is that we learn to recognize how that
works so that we are not deceived.

An analogy may help to make the point. James Barr was once asked why it was necessary for seminary students to learn Greek and Hebrew. In those days, that was a hot issue, somewhat more so the farther down you went on the grading scale. Barr's answer is the best I have ever heard to that question. You should learn Greek and Hebrew, he said, not to be able somehow to get at the "real meaning" of a text, as though fully accurate translation were impossible. And not even to be able to fathom the recondite subtleties of thought form or perceptual style that may be built into the Greek or Hebrew tongues. No, Barr said, in fact one can live quite happily without knowing Greek and Hebrew, *if* one recognizes that not knowing them places a limit on what you can claim you know about a text and recognizes where the limit falls. Knowing that is far more the issue than knowing Greek or Hebrew.

The moral for the preacher's exegesis is similar. It is not a matter of learning how to purge our own agendas from reading a text, so much as it is a matter of knowing the limits of what we bring to a text, and claim to know about it—limits laid down by our humanness, our brokenness, our emotional agendas, and all the rest. It is a matter of being willing to have what we *thought* was an answer turned around and made into a question when we enter the sphere of a text's envitalized experience. In short, the builder chooses tools with a view to the interaction of tool and material, each reacting to the limits and influence of the other.

The second horror of eisegesis is more pragmatic. You have heard it said that you should not find a text to match a sermon topic, but rather let the topic come out of the text. I wonder why? Why is it so taboo to come to the Bible with a need or a thought or a wonderment and to expect meaningful dialogue with scripture's witness? We are not talking about using the Bible as an answer book or anything of the sort. But it seems to be a kind of fearful unfaith to say that the Bible is not sturdy enough to be in the position of speaking second in a conversation we may want to have with it. So long as we are willing to let our original assumptions, queries, and suggestions be trans-

formed by the experience of living in a text we should not fear
"searching the scriptures" *for* something we can already put
into some kind of words.

Probably the most useful and most neglected bibliographical
tool for the preacher at the leading edge of sermon preparation
is a topical concordance of the Bible. The one most available is
an up-dated alphabetical encyclopedia of topics, under which
are cited various biblical texts that have something to do with
each topic.[2] I would far rather a preacher who wants, frankly, to
preach on a topic—let us say, anger and Christian love—take
that concern as a starting point, find a text to join in hermeneutical dialogue, and come out with a sermon rooted and
grounded in the biblical experience, than for the same preacher
to embark on a so-called topical sermon without biblical footing, or still worse, to drag a text in as umpire making the
sermon look biblical on the outside without the richness of
biblical witness on the inside. Faithful eisegesis is far to be
preferred, on theological grounds, than careless or routinized
exegesis. Or, to sit lightly to some otherwise serious language,
if a preacher has to go around in circles to prepare a sermon,
let it be the hermeneutical circle of conversation with a text
rather than the vicious one of applying uninterpreted scripture
to unchallenged thought.

Chapter 6. **Over- and Underpreparation**

We all know of the superdedicated preacher who spends one
hour in preparation for every one minute of preaching. As
things get heated up in the parish, that is a little tarnished as an

objective, but it can still get a good show of humble and envious amazement from an audience of working preachers. No one has ever said that it was just plain crazy, but it is. (Then again, one could say that no agency has ever rewarded obsessional behavior so lavishly and theologically as the Christian church through the ages, but that is another story.) Oddly enough, your one-hour-per-minute sermon is quite likely to be underprepared, and for contrast, your humbler Saturday night special may be overprepared. Here is how it happens.

Every well-trained preacher's library contains Bible commentaries in one form or another—*Interpreter's Bible* for the timid, *International Critical Commentary* for the zealous, and all points in between. It is standard practice in teaching homiletics to direct preaching students to commentaries early on in sermon preparation. It is equally standard practice for this dedicated dependence on commentaries to be worn as the scholarly badge of the journeyman preacher who has "kept up" despite the maelstrom of parish work. Now, there is nothing wrong with commentaries, no matter how dull they are, *except that they are not primarily tools for sermon preparation.* A sermon whose author has slaved for hours over the commentaries is likely to be as overprepared and tough as bread that was kneaded twice too long.

And the second is like unto the first: a sermon that has not fermented in the vat of its author's struggle, imagination, and interpretation is underprepared no matter how many hours were clocked on it. In a word, preachers have a tendency to depend too obsessively and too long on commentaries and secondary materials and to brood and imagine too fearfully and too little about what way a text or subject is trying to have with them. So you get the paradoxical and embarrassing situation of a sermon you just know had twenty hours behind it landing dead as a doornail as any kind of invitation to the Bible's world of transcendent presence, while the half-finished product of someone's insight while strap-hanging between subway stops soars like an eagle with its hearers close behind.

There is no mystery here and no magic. Nor is there any license for slipshod and neglectful preparation. Instead, there is an affirmation of the central importance of the preacher's creative encounter and struggle with a text as the nursery of faithful preaching. Lots of good books have been written about that.[1] The best of them are a call to responsible involvement on the preacher's part and have little patience with narcissistic flights of fantasy, half-baked rappings, and clever formulizing. Adequate preparation is always harder work than either over- or underpreparing, no matter how long in minutes that preparation takes. It is time, in other words, we stopped looking at the clock to arbitrate the adequacy of our study and consulted the intensity and depth of our own flawed interpretation instead.

Yes, there is a place for commentaries. It is somewhere *after* a preacher has lived inside a text long enough at least to have a tourist visa. Commentaries, especially those which emphasize literary, linguistic, and geographical aspects of a text, are useful for checking up on one's own interpretation, for reminding us of oddities and obstacles we might otherwise skip over, and not least for reminding us that centuries of tradition and wisdom lie between us and the eventfulness of what we preach. All well and good. Commentaries may clarify the text as a message; they do not deliver the text as an invitation to meaning.

One kind of printed resource that is almost universally neglected, however, is a good book on biblical geography. The Bible is an earthy book, even in its most rarified theological sections, and there is hardly a text in it that does not in some measure depend for its intelligibility on a reader's knowledge of the *scene* of the writing—political, economic, environmental, geographical. Preachers would do well to cultivate the curiosity of their favorite detective or superspy: an insatiable skepticism about the ordinariness of every detail in a scene. What was that dish's function? How many roads led into that little town, and what kind of traffic did they carry? What would the rest of a village normally be doing at that hour of the day? If you had been walking in sandals all day, how did you get a bath? What was the pecking order of agricultural hired help in those days? What sort of political clout did that kind of Jewish official have? What topics of conversation were not allowed in polite society? And so it goes. The list of "geographical" details is endless. Not that all that information is going to appear in a sermon, of course, but you can hardly overdo your immersion in the actual scene of the text.

An encounter I had with a preaching student last year illustrates the difference between getting into the scene and indenturing yourself to a commentary. This particular student had a natural gift for scene setting in his sermons. He just gravitated effortlessly to a rich, vivid, accurate description of what it was like in, through, and around the text of his sermon. He was to preach twice in the class I taught, and the first sermon unmistakably showed his talent for scene setting. The time came for his second sermon some weeks later, which to my and his fellow students' horror was lethal—supernaturally dull, as one English bishop is supposed to have said of a colleague. Every commentary known to humankind must have been consulted, and most managed at least a walk-on line in what was supposed to have been a sermon. After the obstacle course of boring obfuscation he put us through, I asked what in heaven's name had happened to his facility for involving us so completely in a biblical scene. Oh, he confessed, when he first wrote the second sermon it was full of such detail. But he had shown it to a biblical instructor as part of an exegesis course, and the instructor had told him that stuff didn't belong in sermons and to use the commentaries for some "meat" instead.

In effect, the fascination with geographical detail was the student's own way into a creative involvement with the text. It would not be everyone's. The point is that with his second sermon he had labored longer and to less result because through the commentaries he stayed on the outside of the text looking in. His second sermon was vastly more overprepared and considerably less effective than his first, to say nothing of the surplus hours he had put into it.

An aside is in order just about here concerning those inevitable times in the preparation of sermons when we are just plain stuck—half in and half out, so to speak, with no way in sight to make any sensible completion of a sermon we thought had started out fine. What do you do then? The answer is easier on, say, a Thursday morning than on Saturday night, but the principle is the same: *when you do not know what to do next, do not do anything.* Go read a novel, or take a walk, or play with the kids, or run the church mimeograph machine. Give whatever part of your brain it is whose business is creativity a chance to work. One of the things we know about creative experience is that it always involves some form of getting stuck and then putting the problem out of mind as the gateway to insight, creative resolution, answer, or what have you.[2] One suspects that some of those one-hour-for-every-minute types would be infinitely better off both as human beings and as preachers if they would learn to recognize the need for a creative "pause" when they met one.

All of us should learn that about ourselves: How does our creative capacity work? What kinds of patterns does it follow? When is getting stuck in preparation a signal that it is time to take off and let go for now, and when do we need to persevere a while longer? It can be a tricky business, and there is no technique to learn for it. What it takes is getting acquainted with one's own way of thinking and creating, one's own hermeneutical strategy so to speak. The basic tool of hermeneutics is neither commentary nor ancient language; it is knowing how your own mind works.

You can think of this overall concern as a matter of construction sequence—knowing what phase of work has to be done at what time in the ecology of your own imagination. Without that self-knowledge, sermons come out looking like an amateur mason's backyard barbeque: so overprepared it could be a flying

buttress, and so underprepared it will not cook a decent marsh-
mallow.

Chapter 7. **Overworked Concreteness**

There is hardly a more venerable injunction in the preaching
business than "Keep your sermons concrete." Abstraction is to
be avoided like the plague. Even laypeople have picked up the
refrain, and who among us has not heard at the church door
some postsermon advice such as "That was fine, preacher, but
how do we apply it concretely?"

In this chapter, I am introducing yet another nontraditional
idea: concreteness is often overworked in preaching; abstraction is often what we should be striving for. This advice is not,
let us hasten to add, a license for woolly thinking or obfuscation. It merely asks us to take seriously in preaching what we do
not hesitate to affirm in education: that the capacity to think
abstractly is the goal of cognitive development and the mark of
adult mental competence. Why is it that something so universally scorned as "abstraction" in preaching seems to be so valued
educationally?

Who knows where the fault lies or just when it happened, but
somewhere along the line homiletics took out after the wrong
enemy. My guess is that what we wanted to affirm was the need
for preaching to involve its listeners in a story of momentous
import for them, the "sacred story" of Jesus' life, death, and
resurrection played out in all the incarnate minutiae of our own
mundane existence. Anything that threatened to veil or dimin-
ish or deflect the kerygmatic encounter of God with humankind
was anathema—as well it should have been. But as in faith we
began to clarify our commitment to the incarnational dimen-

sion of preaching, its promise that nothing less than encounter with transcendence was offered, we made a horrible mistake.

We decided, not suddenly or calculatedly, but slowly and surely, that the kind of involvement we wanted from our listeners in the preaching that for many is nothing less than another of the mighty acts of God, was to be identified with something like our hearers' *attentiveness*. From that it quickly became obvious, particularly in America after the great awakenings that continue to happen either locally or across the continent, that what was calculated to hold the attentive interest of our listeners was whatever had directly to do with their lives at the most immediate pressure point. The pulpit played its part in the anti-intellectualism of American life documented so ably by Richard Hofstadter.[1] Immediacy was therefore good because it gripped and held people's attention; remoteness was bad. We began to lose our capacity in communication to "suspend judgment," to defer gratification in the name of some longer-range purpose or more far-reaching goal. We wanted the payoff *now*.

Still the mistake was not fatal. Had concepts such as immediacy versus remoteness gone into the homiletical canon, things would be far different today. Somewhere, though, the concepts changed so that immediacy became *concreteness,* and remoteness turned into *abstraction.* Time has added to the concepts, but their core is the same. Ask a homiletician, and he or she will likely tell you that concreteness means such things as ease of comprehension, ready applicability to everyday life, simplicity of utterance, and even fidelity to the model of Jesus' own preaching, which was down to earth, easy to get, concrete. In the metamorphosis of terms, however, we slipped a cog: *immediacy* and *remoteness* are functional, dynamic terms; *concreteness* and *abstraction* are rhetorical, linguistic ones. Ever since, we have tried to meet a functional, dynamic need for immediacy with a rhetorical, linguistic criterion of concreteness, and it has never really worked.

What we forgot in preaching was what developmental psychology, among other areas of inquiry, was just beginning to learn: that the human ability to cope with the stresses and strains of even normal, let alone traumatic, existence increases directly with our capacity to tolerate wider circles of ambiguity, to delay our wish for an answer until more of the problem has unfolded, to use and understand symbols that are one or more steps removed from direct representation of the objects or events that lie behind them, in short, to think abstractly precisely in order to be free from the tyranny of misplaced or premature concreteness. Most preachers trained in the modern era know something of Jean Piaget and his famous work with children's cognitive development.[2] Most of those preachers know and agree that the growth of the mind is toward the adult capacity for "formal operations" (in Piaget's language) as the mark of mature thinking capability. Formal operations are abstract processes. What separates me from my very bright seven-year-old son is not really a fund of information, and certainly not something like "intelligence," but is rather precisely the difference that as an adult I can think abstractly (about principles, connections, relationships, and implications that are clear as abstract ideas), while the child cannot yet do that. I can think of the evil of robbery; my son thinks of the meanness of robbers.

There is more. Every working day of their lives, pastors make good use of the idea that adults need to be able to function more, not less, abstractly in order to cope with life. The power of abstraction, then, is not in service to remoteness but rather the reverse: it serves to allow a meaningful and competent involvement in the intricacies and immediacies of existence. When theodicy becomes a searing personal issue, not a theological oddity, it is not the concreteness of a maimed body that we look to, but the abstract promise of a God still in control even when the concrete evidence is damning. When the church budget committee wants to keep the money concretely at home so we can see where it goes, we see our ministry as helping them value the abstract idea of mission, of sending money off to someplace where we can no longer see and feel it.

The moral is that in most ways we seek to cultivate people's capacity for dealing with abstraction, knowing that both the

concept and the aim are appropriate. When we come to speak
of preaching, though, we fear that very thing we seek to cultivate
elsewhere. It is a painful contradiction.

One of the best illustrations of what is at stake here comes not
from preaching but from the world of psychotherapy. Sheldon
Kopp writes of a patient who slowly came to give up her neurot-
ic dependence on parents who, in fact, had never offered her
even the basic emotional nutrients for growth. Listen to his
description of her experience:

> The core reactions to that [parental] deprivation were rage, grief,
> and helplessness. These had to be faced, a bit at a time, as she felt
> ready for each new disclosure [in therapy]. Tortured episodes of
> recognition and release were always followed by the interludes of
> rest and withdrawal that she needed to begin to integrate each new
> disclosure. *The spiraling course of her reentry and retreat deepened with each
> new sweep of expanding consciousness.*[3]

Kopp's helical image of continual "sweeps" of growing awareness is every bit as good for preaching as it is for psychotherapy.[4] The capacity for abstraction, or greater sweeps of
consciousness, is far from being the enemy of good preaching.
It is closer to being its goal.

It was a layperson rather than a minister or academician who
introduced me to the idea that preaching's long-term results
are the ones worth looking for. A woman in a small-town south-
ern church was commenting one day on old Dr. So-in-so who
had been the pastor for years and years in the church I was then
serving. He was not a terribly good preacher in any one sermon, she said, but when she stopped to think about listening to
him preach week in and week out for years on end, she realized
she had gotten a complete theological education without knowing it. Few of us preachers think in terms of what we aim to
accomplish in our preaching taken over a very long haul. From
a communicative point of view, however, it is precisely this
regular and sustained "exposure" of our people to our preaching that counts. *It is in the longitudinal perspective that abstraction*

proves to be not an enemy but a goal. In that long haul, we may hope to enable people to range more widely and more confidently in the world of their consciousness, to reach out farther and farther into the unknown realms of experience that are accessible once we are free of the oppressive tyranny of "concreteness" used as it usually is in discussions of preaching.

The really important thing is for a preacher to have some basic understanding and empathy for where the people are in terms of their capacity to think reflectively and abstractly *and then* to lead them progressively beyond their present situation. Almost every book on preaching says the first part; we need help with the last, too. The preacher's strategic stance should always be a tensive one—slightly in advance, asking and enabling the people to move forward bit by bit. When we protest against sermons that are "too abstract," what we probably really mean is that the creative distance between sermon and people is too great, and they are left behind. *What we fail to realize is that communication suffers just as much when a sermon is not abstract enough.* Studies of human information processing have found that our handling of messages reaches a peak when the complexity of the message is optimal for the people hearing it.[5] "Optimal" in these studies meant stretching them a little, but not too much, and not too little either. The moral to this otherwise complex and fascinating area of investigation is pretty direct for preaching: it *is* after all possible for a sermon to be too concrete, too far behind the creative distance needed for people to grow and develop.

Chapter 8. **Preaching for Yourself**

Along with a renewed interest in pastoral care in the last generation of ministers came a renewed emphasis on preaching to

people's needs. Not only was biblical faithfulness imperative for
preaching, so too was being in touch with human lives on a
pastoral basis. To this day, we tell preaching students that they
will not find a really comfortable method for preaching until
they get into a parish or other ministerial context where their
pastoral relationships with people give them the catalytic
experience through which the gospel comes alive in human
words. And we mean it. But we are sometimes in danger of
becoming romantic about "preaching to people's needs." For
one thing, a whole houseful of people are likely to have pretty
different needs. For another, we run the recurring risk of trying
to force a biblical text or theological concept into sermons that
fit them only by the longest stretch of the eisegetical imagination. After all, one thing the Bible does is *define* needs otherwise
unclear.

So we must add another piece of advice to students and
ministers: *preach to and for yourselves.* If you as pastors are truly
living the lives of your people, if you are tuning into their own
situations and making them your own, then you should trust
that what concerns you as their pastor is also their concern.
Preach to that. Let that enter into hermeneutical dialogue with
text and topic. Use yourselves as hermeneutical tools, as points
of intersection between human reality and biblical word. A
Swiss pastor tells of a traumatic learning experience just on this
subject. He found himself obliged to call on an acutely depressed young woman. She lay in her bed silent and uncom-
municative.

At the end of his visit, he took his pocket New Testament out (as
he still felt he had to do) and opened it. Two days before he had been
at a party for children during which he had been caught in a battle
of confetti. Later, he had carefully picked the confetti out of his hair,
from his suit and his pockets. But he had forgotten to check his
pocket Testament, and when he opened it to read some passages to
the woman, a shower of confetti rained upon her bed. After an
anxious and flustered moment, the minister burst into laughter, and

the woman couldn't help but laugh too. The prayer and the Scripture reading that were supposed to follow were forgotten. The ridiculous ending of his pastoral visit had accomplished more than the most dignified and serious meditation could have done.[1]

From the world of pastoral counseling and psychotherapy comes the fundamental rule for helpers: when you listen to a person in need, pay attention to your own feelings, fantasies, and thoughts, for they are your most direct route to the inner life of the person you are hearing. It is time preachers took the same advice. That does not mean, as you might have guessed, sticking to the safe subjects with which you yourself have gained a comfortable security. Far from it. Preaching for yourself means that you preach about the question marks, the uncertainties, the shifting loyalties, the blurry road markers of whatever pilgrimage you are making. I wonder why it so often is that we insist on a measure of "closure" for our sermons that we never dream of achieving for our own reflection. Sermons have to end, we say, and it is best to leave people on a positive note with as many loose ends as possible wrapped up. Yet most of us can look back to find some of our best-received sermons were precisely those which did not end neatly, which more matched the incompleteness of our own faith and development. We should trust that experience, because it is telling us something fundamental about the communication process. No amount of false confidence will be able to override the unconscious but strikingly clear message that we do not truly know what we are talking about. The companion dictum is that an honest sharing of struggle is more communicative and more faithful than any escape into fictitious certainty could ever be.

Just here, of course, rises an objection and a serious one. Is not the basic content of preaching the objective Word of God that does not depend on my puny level of understanding? Surely we are not to inflict on our people all our problems and distortions! After all, being genuine about having nothing to say still leaves nothing said, does it not? How can baring my heart possibly help anyone who needs reassurance and support?

Two things need to be said and explained a little. First, what we have been talking about is very far indeed from a gratuitous wallowing in one's own doubts and uncertainties. We are talking about the hermeneutical interaction of preacher and text or topic. Second, for preachers to think they somehow "proclaim" the objective Word of God is theological nonsense, and always has been. Karl Barth, who is often mistakenly invoked on the side of objective proclamation, is probably the foremost critic of preachers who delude themselves into thinking they have some direct and continuous communicative relationship with transcendence. No, what we have to offer is precisely our struggle to do what is impossible to do—preach the Word of God—and it is time we acknowledged that principle at the level of communication dynamics as well as in theological discourse.

What we preachers do at our best is create a *communication environment* in which people may find themselves in the midst of what H. H. Farmer called the "moment of the God–man encounter."[2] We do not create the moment any more than we command God's appearance, although we do things to facilitate it just as we attempt to prepare ourselves for transcendent encounter through worship and ethics. Our own hermeneutical experience provides the equipment for creating that environment, both consciously and unconsciously.

A major part of the sermon's work is accomplished, then, not by displaying the well-crafted results of our struggle to understand and be faithful, but by demonstrating the struggle itself. (We will come back to that from a slightly different angle later on.) Laypeople have been trying to tell us that for years, without much success. It is when the process of growing in faith is shown in the preaching that the preaching connects with the similar strivings of its hearers, bringing them hope, understanding, and comradeship in the battle. To think that I can set before my people the mighty acts of God, or that I can in some way broker the meeting of God with his people through what I say is a lot of obnoxious theological things, starting with pride and ending somewhere near idolatry. But to use my humanness as a seeker after God's will as the strategic foundation for preaching is "incarnational" in its own appropriate theological sense. If the sacrament of the Lord's Supper shows forth the brokenness of Christ for us, then the preached word also can show forth—not prattle about—the struggling faithfulness of response.

For some, that will be a shift in thinking. A similar shift took place in the practice of psychiatry through the influence of Harry Stack Sullivan, whose almost legendary success in treating schizophrenic patients makes him one of the giants of modern psychiatry and psychotherapy. Sullivan's contribution was not so much theoretical (he never wrote a book, although his reconstructed lectures were published posthumously by students) as it was personal. Against the traditional notion that therapists were healthy people who helped other people because of their healthiness, Sullivan frankly admitted his own unhealth and used his own struggle for emotional balance and well-being as his single most effective therapeutic tool. Virtually singlehandedly, Sullivan changed the thinking of generations of therapists to come. Using oneself in one's own struggle for health is what allows us to help other people, not claiming a finished-ness and equillibrium we never had to begin with.

Seward Hiltner has written lightly but movingly on the minister in the role of clown.[3] The clown is the character who makes us laugh in the circus, yes; but more than that it is the clown who by being so flagrantly human in its maladroitness keeps us from being overwhelmed by the virtuosity of the other performers. It is as though the mundaneness of the clown tames the frightening otherness of the transcendent high-flyers and frees us to gaze on the holy without being consumed. So too, the preacher. When we preach for ourselves, we allow, clownlike, those who look to us similarly to confess their humanness and open themselves to the work of God from which they otherwise shrink in fear.

To shift the image: I once served a church in a southwestern region noted for its subterranean limestone caverns. One of the most majestic of these underground palaces had been discovered haphazardly by two small boys on a hike through the woods, who found a small opening and wondered what was down there. The preacher is like that. We are not the ones who explore the cave, or lead guided tours, or study its geology, so much as we are the hikers through life who perhaps are gifted with spotting holes in the ground that fellow hikers might have missed, and asking, "I wonder what's down there?"

Chapter 9. **Relevance May Be Irrelevant**

Mercifully, we seem to be past the time when *relevance* was almost a code word for "ultimate goodness." The idea and the problem linger, though, of designing sermons that connect with people's interests and concerns—that are relevant. We still choose illustrations, for example, largely with a view to making what we consider the meat of a sermon, its conceptual structure, palatable to hearers, to make it relevant. The pressure from within and without the preaching business is to be sure sermons have a practical application, a demand that can send preachers into a frenzy of activity to be certain, week in and week out, that Jesus scourging the money changers has something to do with the rising cost of gasoline.

No one seems to have thought that the tremendous energy we spend on trying to be relevant in preaching might also be a backhanded slap in the face to congregations. It may mean we do not give them much credit for being able to make theological connections themselves or for being able to puzzle out on their own how the content of a sermon might include them. Obviously, we do not want a contest of wits, with preachers teasing listeners to see how remote they are willing to let our sermons be before walking out after the first act. But it should be just as obvious that if we have to *make* an idea relevant when it was not to begin with we should not be preaching it in the first place.

Plenty of experience and research have accumulated to show that people by and large do what is genuinely expected of them. When little is expected, little is given; when much is expected, people rise to the occasion. It works that way in education, in industry, in counseling. Why should it be any different in preaching? One of the best-kept secrets of homiletics is that people are *trying* to make connections between what the preacher says and where they live. It takes a strange twist of logic to imagine that people come back again and again if they find it so devilishly difficult to see themselves in sermons, to make connections between preaching and living, or to find any practical use for the theological meanderings of their preacher. It is truer to say that people will be allies and fellow participants in the preaching task *if that is what is expected of them.*

What is expected of them depends, in turn, to a large extent on what their preacher *says* is expected of them, both directly and indirectly. Illustrations that are explained to death say to people that not much is expected of their imaginations. Sermons that always answer all questions and leave nothing uncertain say to people that not much is expected of their tolerance for the ambiguities of life. Preaching that tries to oversimplify even the complexities of life says to people that not much is expected of their minds. Sermons as concrete as sidewalks may be remarkably easy to listen to, but they also say that remarkably little confidence is placed in their hearers' capacities to think.

Now, it can be said, probably correctly, that our congregations on the whole are biblically illiterate, theologically naive, and religiously impoverished. It would seem that little *could* be expected of them. It is a vicious circle, all right, but perhaps we ought to ask whether working so hard for relevance tightens or loosens the noose. If we have tried unsuccessfully to break that circle by working so hard to be relevant and "meet people where they are," perhaps it is time to go the other direction and expect more of people in order to lead them someplace else. Paul Scherer used to say that the trouble with preaching to people where they are is that they are usually in the wrong place.

A highly personal, but quite pervasive, attitude among preachers seems to lie beneath the relevance problem. Although it is often unconscious, the attitude of many preachers toward their listening congregations seems to be adversarial rather than collegial. That is, we very subtly put ourselves into the position of working against a congregation's resistance, or trying to overcome its disinterest, or seeking to avoid its displeasure. We look on its members in covert and unadmitted ways as adversaries rather than as colleagues in our struggle to discover and act out the truth in Jesus Christ. "How long can I preach before they lose interest? Have I repeated my points so they don't get confused? Have I got one illustration for each point so they don't think it's too abstract? Does my introduction get their attention and make them receptive? Is my language simple enough that they won't get restless? Have I been ginger enough with controversial issues so they won't get mad? Have I been entertaining enough so they'll come back next week?" And so it goes through the working preacher's catechism of "effectiveness," based almost entirely on the supposition that preaching has to work against the natural drift of a congregation instead of with it. The noose tightens: we expect resistance, and get it; we do not ask people to be fully accredited participants in the preaching task, and we wind up alone and exhausted.

Where the adversarial attitude comes from is hard to say. Lots of people have lots of different ideas. One of the most insightful is based on the idea of resistance talked about in psychotherapeutic circles, and it goes like this: the closer we get to things that really matter to people deep down, the more intense a reaction we can expect. Consciously or unconsciously, people will resist anything that looks like tampering with the most basic values of their lives, whatever they are. Or, as the biblical picture so graphically displays it, the demons that take up residence in us never give up without a struggle. Preachers have been hitting resistance so long they chronically have their guard up.

But if that is correct, then preachers should be clear about one major thing: *resistance is more likely a sign of relevance than of irrelevance.* As James Dittes puts it, when we encounter genuine resistance that is not a matter just of the situation or of personality clash, that means we are somehow hitting home or close to it.[1] People can get fed up with irrelevance, it is true. But the resistance we sense in preaching may also be a sign that what we are saying matters a great deal and is too "relevant" to be handled easily. On balance, I vote for giving the latter interpretation a try far more than we have in the past. We sometimes do not realize just how powerful the stuff of preaching really is. We preachers are so used to fearing ourselves to be powerless that we do not recognize the actual potency of much of what we say. We trigger a kind of protective resistance in people, not because we are missing the mark but because we are coming too close to it with too much too soon. The more worried we get about whether what we have to say matters to anyone, the more apt we are to go overboard into resistance in our quest for relevance.

A pastor once undertook to train his deacons to make pastoral calls on people. The deacons had expressed a willingness to visit the flock, and showed some enthusiasm for learning how to do it well. At the first training session, the pastor announced a role play, in which the deacons would take turns playing the roles of caller and callee, in order to get some insight and practice about visitation. The pastor himself led off to break the ice with the slightly nervous deacons. He played the role of deacon-caller, and made every mistake in the book so as to reassure the others that it was all right to show what they did not know, and to illustrate the common errors and pitfalls of calling. The role play went beautifully, but when it was over and the pastor turned to the group for participation, he was met with uneasy, unyielding silence. None of his heroic efforts to salvage the training session worked; the role play had killed it dead. For weeks, he puzzled over how something that seemed so good had fallen so flat. How could something as lively and relevant as a role play have left his deacons so bored and non-participative?

It was only months later, in a discussion with other pastors at a continuing education seminar, that the light finally dawned. He had not failed because he was irrelevant or missing the deacons. The role play failed because it was *too* relevant and hit too close to home for the deacons to handle. His role playing all their possible mistakes and weaknesses had pushed their anxiety level so high that they could do nothing but retreat to protective silence. They probably could not have told him that, because it was largely an unconscious happening. He realized, though, that he had been in a posture of standing over against his deacons, subtly and unwittingly, rather than with them. By underestimating the power of his own communication, and undervaluing their willingness to make connections for themselves, he had overwhelmed them, and it had looked for all the world as though he just had not "reached" them at all. A much larger amount of our preaching than we have realized falls into precisely the same trap.

What we are dealing with here is not so much a matter of technique or the contents of any one sermon as it is an overall strategy for preaching. That is where the problem arises, and that is where it can be solved. Instead of trying to figure out how to make a sermon relevant to people (who, we sometimes think cagily to ourselves, are not much to be trusted to their own devices) we should instead try to envision a people trying in whatever ways they can to make connections between their lives and the good news of Jesus Christ. Yes, they often miss the point. Yes, they are limited in what they can say about themselves or about the Bible. And yes, they often dig in their heels when the going gets too rough. But, as Fosdick hears Paul saying in that memorable sermon to Titus, "For this cause left I thee in Crete."[2] For a change, let us think of these people as people who on the whole are trying to be more faithful, not less; people who will all things considered make better colleagues than adversaries in the preaching task, if we honestly give them the chance. We need, in short, to keep in mind the ironic twist that our nervous attempts to *make* relevance may, down deep, be triggering the very resistance we try so warily and at times so angrily to overcome.

III

SPECS AND MATERIALS
The Tactics of Preaching

"Specs and materials" is the term builders use to describe the architectural specifications and the construction materials they will use in a project. We are now getting down to the business of building the sermon itself, talking about its tactics in a more specific way. In a sense, we preachers have ideas and language as our specs and materials. How the ideas form, relate to each other, and develop in the communication environment is, you could say, the basic architecture of preaching. The way language operates, in turn, is like the erection of the building itself. Those two areas will be the concern of this section, culminating in a critical view of the preaching task from the perspective of diagnosis—what the architect and builder bring to their work as the foundation of its design and development.

Chapter 10. **The Magic Number 7**

We have all chuckled uneasily at the caricature of the dimwitted but sincere parson who only has three ideas to his name and preaches them all in rotation, week in and week out. We chuckle because it is so comic; we are uneasy because it is so close to the truth, which is that most of us do not have more than a handful of basic ideas nor should we be expected to. Here is the way it works.

A fascinating research project was undertaken in which the objective was to learn how people perceived and categorized their worlds.[1] That is, assuming that we have to have some way of organizing and making sense of the vast bombardment of sensations we get every waking moment, what kinds of pigeonholes do human beings have for sorting out what they experience? What basic ideas, concepts, images, orientations, or what have you do we use in order literally to "make" sense out of what would otherwise be a blur of what our senses and minds serve up for our consumption? And how many such basic pigeonholes might we ordinarily have anyway?

The answer turned out to be none other than the magic number 7, which throughout human history has traditionally had a special place and significance in the ways of the world, especially the religious world. More precisely, investigators found that virtually all people think in terms of seven separate categories (plus or minus two) about any one thing at any one time. For instance, if we are asked to listen to a series of musical tones of varying pitches, and to sort those sounds into separate groups that seem to be the same, we will come up over and over again with seven groupings, plus or minus two. It is no accident that there are a limited number of tones in the musical scale. The same holds for color hues, and it is no accident again that the spectrum we see has seven separate colors. Now of course we can subdivide any group into still more separate groups, but we almost never get beyond the seven, plus or minus two, in any *one* sorting process.

Perhaps that is no more than a complicated way of getting to what Faulkner is supposed to have said, that all the world's wisdom can be expressed in six clichés. The moral for the preacher follows: we arrange and organize our thinking into a limited number of categories. It is a fact of human nature that overall we do not have more than seven, plus or minus two, truly basic ideas about the universe. We are creatures with almost limitless capacity for subdivision of those categories, and the novelty, the texture, the stimulation of being alive comes with that capacity. But when we push back to basics about something, the magic number 7, plus or minus two, is our lot in life.

It needs to be said, then, that the working life of a preacher consists not so much in dreaming up new ideas for sermons, as in creating themes and variations on a small number of basic ideas about the world that give each of us our particular world view or "standpoint" for reality as Michael Novak says.[2] Preachers can use that fact of life more than they have.

For one thing, knowing that we think in limited numbers of categories gets us off the hook of thinking we have to keep producing endless new ideas for preaching. Ask any seminary student just learning to preach, and you are almost bound to discover some amount of anxiety over how in the world he or she will have anything new to *say* every week for God knows how many more years! About all we can say to them is that somehow it works out in practice. The *way* it works we can now identify. Given a basic small number of themes, preaching consists of variation after variation.

Aside from relieving us of some bewilderment about the seemingly impossible task of dreaming up that many new ideas, the magic number 7 gives us two invaluable aids we did not know we had: a way of checking up on ourselves, and a way of planning pulpit work.

The way of checking up on ourselves is simple but effective.

If we can identify the fundamental themes of our preaching, we can ask whether we have gotten stuck on any one or more themes and sold ourselves short in the having-something-to-say department, or whether we need to rethink and revamp our basic approach to theological thinking. Chapter 18 suggests a concrete way of making an inventory of our basic ideas by looking at a sample of our past sermons. Each preacher's way of formulating his or her inventory will be different, of course, but what allows us to talk to each other and to the tradition we have in common is a large degree of overlap and similarity in our separate inventories. Learning to articulate the basic structure of our preaching ideas is both a way of getting in touch with each other and at the same time a way of occupying our own particular piece of history in which we are unique, creative individuals. It might be interesting, for example, for a preacher to ask how his or her basic ideas and their relative importance or weight differ from and resemble those of the congregation served. It may well be that a lot of what looks like faulty communication or conflict between a preacher and congregation, for instance, is really a different weighting and valuing of fundamental themes, more than it is a disagreement about the truth of any one idea or the particulars of any single action. Keep in mind, too, that we are not talking here about taking sides on issues, but rather about the prior emergence of an issue itself as a thought category.

Not only is the magic number 7 a good checkup tool, it can also be used as a basic resource for sermon planning over a period of time. It probably could be said that most of us at one time or another have every good intention of planning ahead in our preaching, with considerably more emphasis on the intention than on the actual planning. One preacher who was on record as being both enthusiastic and successful as a long-range sermon planner had to confess that the chief motivating force was a bulletin printer's deadline that was four weeks in advance of any particular Sunday!

Even without having to justify our poor performance in the

face of good planning intentions, however, there is something very important to be said about not "canning" sermons so far in advance that a preacher cannot respond to the weekly rhythm, concerns, needs, and events of the congregation. Not planning ahead takes its toll on the preacher in pressure and anxiety, but it also keeps things current in the pulpit. The magic number 7 enters the picture at this point as a way of planning without losing the pastoral spontaneity and currency we want to keep.

Quite simply, once the basic inventory of preaching ideas is made, sermons can be planned to cycle through it, or series of sermons on the various topics of the inventory can be planned, *without necessarily specifying the exact content of particular sermons.* That last seems to say that a preconceived idea comes first and then a text is chosen and a sermon developed to fit into it. What could be more flagrant eisegetical abuse? Well, several things— for one, not being aware of the perspective from which one looks at a particular text, like it or not. We have to keep in mind that we do not have the power to choose *whether* we think in basic categories or not; we do have the power to reflect on *which* categories we are using at a given time and in a given experience. That is to say, the notion that we could empty ourselves before a text and approach it as a *tabula rasa* was never accurate to begin with. Using our inventory of thought categories as a way of selecting texts does not mean "reading into" the text in a way we might otherwise avoid; rather, it means becoming aware of the perspective from which we view a text precisely so we might take due account of the elements of our preunderstanding that are inevitably at work.

In fact, the whole business of choosing a text has always been a troublesome matter. Methods range from letting the Bible fall open at random, St. Francis-style (as the legend goes), to following a lectionary with complete fidelity. One of the basic arguments in favor of using a lectionary has traditionally been that is keeps us "objective" in text selection and prevents us from riding our own hobbyhorses through the scriptures. Unfortunately, no matter how valuable the lectionary might be on other grounds, the traditional argument for using it overlooks one significant item: once a text is selected, there are many different perspectives from which we may read it, depending on our inventory of basic organizing concepts. You could say there are two points at which a preacher's own assumptions and thought categories enter the picture so far as a text is concerned: (1) at the point of selecting a text and (2) at the point of interpreting the text once it is chosen. A lectionary removes the preacher from the first point (or seems to) but never from the second. Only a preestablished or formulized interpretation of a text could do that, and then *it* would have to have had an author with preunderstandings, just as any commentary does.

It may prove to be far more honest to ask preachers to shoulder their responsibilities for self-reflection and awareness of their own values at both points of contact with the text—selection and interpretation. In any event, to assume that because a lectionary has specified a text the preacher is home free, with no further worry about working his or her own agenda, is nonsense.

Conrad Massa has argued that the choice of a text is itself a theological decision of prime importance for preachers, one we commonly overlook in practice and abdicate altogether when we use a lectionary.[3] Lectionaries are commonly thought of as those lists of texts found in books of common worship, prayer books, and the like, with each tradition having its own list of texts by week or day by day. While those things are without doubt lectionaries, it would be a mistake to say that all a lectionary is is one of those things. The idea of a curriculum in education provides a good analogy for how we sometimes misconstrue lectionaries without realizing it. D. Campbell Wyckoff, for many years one of the leading specialists in Christian education curriculum development, has written that a "curriculum" should not be thought of as a particular set of materials, but rather as the organizing principle at work in any educational venture, whether formalized on paper or not.[4] In other words, the way we get things together educationally *is* the curriculum for that particular setting. The books and pamphlets and audiovisuals that we use in Christian education are resources *for* the curriculum, but they are not the curriculum itself.

The same distinction should be made about lectionaries. A lectionary should be thought of as whatever organizing principle is at work in selecting a series of biblical texts for preaching or reading. The lectionary, then, is not precisely that list of texts in the back of the book, but rather is the organizing principle that lies behind the selection of that list. (Oh, to be sure, we use the word two different ways and there is nothing wrong with that, any more than there is any great harm done by calling this quarter's church school materials "the curriculum.") For the most part, that organizing principle remains unstated and mysterious. Sometimes it is a historical scheme going through the salvation history from Adam to John the Divine; sometimes it is based on the church year and its seasons. Specialized lectionaries have been developed based on pastoral themes or even the seasons of nature. The point is that unless we first know the lectionary's underlying scheme, and then agree to follow it into interpretation of texts, we will hardly be able to keep from using our own built-in "lectionary" of thought categories *regardless whether the actual list of texts was given to us or was home-made.* Simply put, the "lectionary" is a flimsy protection from the influence of our own underlying categories of thinking. It might pay to be honest about that from the first.

On the practical side, preachers should be able to select texts that themselves seem most predominantly to be congruent with one thought category or another, and so to develop lectionaries with every bit as much integrity as those already written. Bear in mind that even a random assortment of texts is a lectionary, whose underlying principle was chaos. Knowing what one's inventory of ideas is prevents an unconscious skewing in one direction or another. It allows us to plan consciously and with appropriate self-criticism what would otherwise be planned unconsciously, with the fiction of "objectivity."

Chapter 11. **The Languages of Preaching. I: The Jerusalem Connection**

In many denominations, every minister keeps a biographical dossier on file in the headquarters office, for use by pastoral search committees, public relations people, and the like.[1] The dossier form for my own group asks at one point: "In how many languages can you preach?" Most of us answer, "One." And most of us are wrong.

The fact is, communication in preaching is such a complex experience that to understand it we would do much better to think of several "languages" being spoken even in what seems like ordinary English preaching. Just for openers, there is the language of formal theology ("God's grace forgives sin"), the language of religious experience ("We felt free, in touch with God's presence"), the language of illustration, the language of history, the language of the Bible, the language of everyday happening, the language of feeling, and, of course, the nonverbal language of the body. Like the colored wires of a telephone cable, they are all wrapped up in what *seems* like one thing—plain (we hope) English.

But the preacher, like the telephone installer, has to make the right connections so communication can take place the way we want it to, and heaven help us if green gets spliced to red. Knowing about the different strands and what each does can get to be pretty important. That is our concern in this and the next chapters—learning a little about the different languages of preaching so we can communicate better in the pulpit and so we can understand what happened when it does not always work the way we hoped.

A pastoral counselor who was for many years senior chaplain at a large state mental hospital tells the following true story. One of his saddest "back ward" cases was a Greek schizophrenic, hopelessly out of touch with reality, who had been vegetating in the hospital for years. No one quite knew where the patient had come from, and because it was agreed that he was beyond helping no one paid much attention to him. The chaplain finally arranged for a local Greek Orthodox priest in the community to visit the poor fellow, as much for giving him a chance to speak his native tongue as for pastoral reasons. He had not had a chance to do so for years.

The priest, who was clinically trained, returned somewhat shaken from the visit and nervously asked the chaplain, "What in the world is that fellow doing there? He's as healthy as you and I!" Bit by bit, the tragic but illuminating story was pieced together after all those years. The Greek "schizophrenic" was a sailor who had jumped ship long ago in a nearby port. He had spoken no English at all, had gotten into some sort of trouble and, as still sometimes happens despite our best intentions, was clapped into the mental institution. There he slowly learned English. *But he learned his English from schizophrenic patients.* Now certain language misuse is often characteristic of that form of mental dysfunction, almost diagnostically so.[2] Our poor Greek, therefore, managed to learn completely schizophrenic English. To the English-speaking psychiatrists and workers, he sounded (and in fact acted) schizophrenic, and was every bit as removed from reality as his sickest fellow patients.

The Greek Orthodox priest had conversed with him in Greek, something that had never happened before in the hospital, *and when he spoke Greek the man was perfectly normal.* It can be fairly said that the hospital staff was both humbled and taught by the experience; the Greek "patient," in his turn, was released. I offer that as an illustration of the way language and "reality" are intertwined, to the extent that what sense we make both *of* the world and *to* other people depends heavily on the languages we speak. Crazy in English, sane in Greek.

The same thing happens with preachers whose sanity is unquestioned but who, theologically speaking, become different people altogether when they begin to preach. Let us take the case (again an actual one, suitably disguised) of a Dr. Wordbinder. He is a well-trained clergyman who has kept up his thinking and reading and comes across as very much "on target" theologically. He speaks of the power of the gospel to set people free for deep relationship to God and to their neighbors; he understands the dynamics of love and forgiveness in the full interplay of human emotions; his theology is firmly rooted in the live human experience of openness, mystery, and servanthood that discipleship involves.

But in the pulpit he becomes a theological throwback. His sermons are long, rambling, and obese with theological jargon. His style is alternately aggressive and whining; his illustrations reinforce the most banal pietism of oversimplification. His use of the Bible, despite what he believes and knows, is literalistic, authoritarian, and repressive. His problem, to intermingle our illustrations, is that the green wire got connected to the red one, and the poor man is sane in Greek but crazy in English. The language of his preaching not only conveys a different message from his conviction, but it also involves his listeners in a totally different view of reality—God, humanity, the forces of existence —from what he believes or wants to share.

The tragedy is that Dr. Wordbinder's heartfelt purpose in preaching has been subverted by his language. It is not his sermon organization or his elocution or his feelings that are getting in the way; it is his language itself. Dr. Wordbinder is a more serious case of the type who scowls and growls his or her way through a sermon on love, or the type who thoroughly depresses the whole congregation with a mournful lament about how we have lost our sense of joy.

All this can be summed up in a kind of formula: *language has the power to shape experience.* If different kinds of experience need to be expressed through different kinds of language, then it is also true that different languages have the power to shape different experiences. We preachers ought to be interested in that interplay between language and experience, because by speaking different languages in our preaching we in fact are contributing to our people's correspondingly different experiences of the gospel. Witness our friend Wordbinder, for whom the experience of Christian faith was personally alive and meaningful, but whose pulpit language contributed to a far different experience for his listeners—the farthest thing from the sharing he intended.

But how does a preacher check up on his or her various languages? How do we know if the red and green wires are connected right or not—if our language and preaching are congruent, to use a pastoral concept? Dr. Wordbinder, for instance, probably senses that something is askew in his preaching, but the chances are good he does not know what it is. Can we help him? Yes. Preachers can learn to be aware of the languages of their preaching, and to monitor them in order to use them consistently, intentionally, and effectively. It is time to move from the basic point—that language and the experience of reality are intertwined—to the question of using languages appropriately for the purposes we really intend.

To keep the discussion straight, let us think in terms of two concepts: *connectedness* and *context.* The first will occupy us here, the second in the next chapter. For effective preaching, the languages of preaching must be appropriately connected to the experience they shape and consistent with their context. If we either disconnect or decontextualize them, we are in trouble. If we keep them straight, we ought to be well on the way to doing in preaching what we aim to do as prophets and priests.

The concept of connectedness grows out of some of the most significant work ever done in the area of language development, the earliest research of the famed Swiss developmental psychologist Jean Piaget. Piaget conducted the following experiment with young children ranging in age from four to twelve, in order to determine how their skill in understanding and using language grew.[3] He told his young subjects a simple fairytale, then asked them to retell the same story to others. An eight-year-old, for instance, fed back a garbled version of the story that seemed to indicate he had understood little of it. But when the eight-year-old was questioned in detail about the story it was equally clear that he had understood it perfectly. What had happened?

The problem, Piaget diagnosed, was that the child's "style of talking" was not yet keeping pace with his understanding; he quite literally *knew* more than he could *say*. In retelling the story, the children would omit parts of it, reverse the sexes of characters, interchange roles, and invert sequences of events. The only way you could make sense of the report was to know the story yourself in advance. The children could not be relied on to sense and appreciate what the listener would naturally not know, even though the children understood the story fully. Children could not connect the language with the "experience" of understanding that they wanted to shape in the hearer. Specifically, they lacked the ability to "assume the listener's perspective," and so retelling of the story could be deciphered only if a hearer knew the story to begin with.

The same thing happens every day with adults—more subject to momentary lapses than to developmental failure—who tell stories, relate incidents, or make requests but leave out essential ingredients. We have all heard perfectly good anecdotes hopelessly butchered in the telling by people who seemed to assume, unthinkingly, that their hearers already knew some of the most important lines.

Translated into our present discussion, that is a problem of missed connections in communication. The language is not adequately connected to the experience it tries to shape, because the speaker has not adequately assumed the perspective of the listeners. Let us come a little closer to home. For preachers, a classic and recurring case of missed connections of exactly that sort is the misuse of theological language in preaching. The term "theological language" is code for certain kinds of religious experience coupled with theological interpretation. If one does not already know about the experience or the interpretation, the code makes no sense. The connection between the language and the experience is missed, just as Piaget's children missed the connection between their language and the meaning experience of the story.

To illustrate: imagine a preacher who wants to share with his or her listeners the experience of a felt acceptance and hopeful security in spite of life's setbacks and injustices. The preacher wants to shape an experience of acceptance, or at least the envisioning of one, but in the preaching uses not the language of experience but the language of theology: "grace," "unmerited divine love," "suffering atonement for our sin," "coming to Jesus," "leaving all masters for God," and so forth, depending on one's theological style. Unfortunately, those theological fragments all require one to know something already about the experience of acceptance before they make any sense as language. Or, to put it another way, preachers who use that kind of language may assume they are describing an actual human experience—past or future—when in fact the language does not *describe* at all. It *interprets* certain happenings and feelings, whose description may very well be the missing link of the sermon. The theological language gets connected to thin air, or, worse, to itself.

We really cannot have it both ways. We cannot require prior experience of what we want to communicate in order to communicate it. You may never understand the meaning of the old saying "You can't make a cake without breaking eggs" until you start trying to understand how language works. This seems to be it: you cannot make language work until you "break it open" and understand what connections with experience and with other language are needed to make it work. If you leave language whole, which is what happens when we use theological language when what we really want is the language of experience, we miss the connections necessary for making sense and shaping experience.

Piaget's discovery was crucial for the preacher. To communicate effectively requires that the communicator be able to assume the listener's perspective, which is almost never that of formal theology or even biblical imagery, in order to know what connections have to be made in the message. In ordinary human communication, that ability comes more or less naturally, with occasional boosts from the educational enterprise. For some reason, though, when we set about the task of formal communication, with messages prepared in advance and delivered in highly structured settings, our natural skill deserts us. Come to think of it, a good deal of training in communication skill really comes down to trying to recover what students ordinarily do quite effectively until they begin thinking actively about it. Unfortunately a lot of preaching is in the same category as the badly told anecdote with its missing links. Some examples:

- Raising an emotional question but providing an intellectual answer;
- Using biblical texts to prove a point without saying why they are authoritative for us, if they are;
- Calling for decision without recognizing what choices we are deciding among;
- Giving an illustration but not saying what it illustrates;
- Arguing for the importance of an answer without saying what was the importance of the question;
- Switching event sequences so that God's action has no stated relationship to human need;
- Using theological abstractions as though they were concrete, witnessable events (God's will, forgiveness, divine mercy or judgment, and so forth);
- Assuming an unstated understanding of faith in order to persuade people to make a commitment of faith—or vice versa.

When adults consistently *cannot* take the role of another, we call it a form of character disorder; when preachers consistently *do not* do it, it is just bad preaching. Listeners come away with the frustrating feeling they should know something they do not, and the gospel in its full, lived sense remains one of the church's best-kept secrets.

What to do about it? Two suggestions. First, preachers should go through their sermons thoroughly and ask themselves over and over again, "What am I *assuming* my listener already knows or has experienced in order for this to make sense?" The results may surprise you. They will also force you to take very seriously the individual characteristics of different audiences. What is assumable for one audience may not be for another.

Second, we should go through our sermons and search religiously for biblical and theological language, God-talk, and then paraphrase in ordinary language each and every instance of it. Notice I do not say "detheologize it" but, rather, "translate it into common, nonreligious speech." In short, you have to break the eggs. Poor Wordbinder, you recall, could not bring himself to do that. When he climbed into the pulpit, he left behind his ability to take the role of his listeners, and his language got disconnected from the experience of the gospel he desperately wanted to shape.

But what happens when you go through your sermon and discover that you simply cannot translate your theological language into the language of experience? What if you cannot get the eggs broken, no matter what? Let us of course leave room for the appropriate and irreducible "oddity" of religious speech, as Ian Ramsey so vividly reminds us.[4] What we are talking about is by no means a campaign to drain theological language of its mystery or of the peculiar metaphoric power it has in what Paul Ricoeur describes as its "semantic impertinence."[5] No, what we are talking about is the situation, all too common in preaching, where language is functioning semantically and communicatively as though it were ordinary dis-

course, when in fact of course it is not that at all. Then you may
have a particular kind of communication malady, the problem
of "verbal realism," which is more widespread than you might
think.[6]

As human beings develop from an infantile to a more mature
understanding of the world, they make an important, although
usually unnoticed, discovery: *words and things are different.* That
is to say, the sign of a thing or of an event is not the same thing
as the thing or event itself—something most of us would yawn-
ingly agree to as among the most obvious of everyday assumptions. For the child, though, and sometimes for adults in certain
ways, it is not only *not* an obvious assumption, it is not even
true. Word and thing *are* the same.

That mixup is called "verbal realism," the confusing business
of thinking that a word itself carries or contains the reality of
the thing it represents. For ready-to-hand examples, you can
tune into the conversation of very young children. My three-
year-old son was quite concerned about robbers. The family car
was broken into about that time and its contents stolen, and my
son's preoccupation with robbery was all the more intensified.
He talked about robbers at great length, demanding to know
why they stole, how we could be safe from them, what kinds of
people they were, and so forth. Suddenly, in the midst of conversation, he stopped short, thought seriously for a few
minutes, and then asked in a very worried way, "If we *talk* about
robbers, will robbers *come?*" Over and over again we assured
him that talking about robbers would not make them come, all
to no avail. (The next day some progress had been made. He
announced to the family that robbers would come only if we
talked about them *a lot.* Some verbose preachers seem to have
found the same solution for the Kingdom of God.) For the
three-year-old, there is not much distance between the talking
and the happening; he was in the middle of verbal realism, just
where he should have been at that age.

Vestiges of verbal realism hang on even into adult life. All too
many adults, for instance, carry traces of the conviction that

feeling or thinking something "inside" carries the same consequences as making it happen in the real world outside. They feel that negative or tabooed feelings are therefore dangerous and to be avoided. That trace of verbal realism is a common hurdle to be overcome in various forms of psychotherapy and counseling. Feeling murderously angry with your wife or supervisor is a very different thing from acting on it; but the difference is sometimes hard to come by.

Another trace of verbal realism brings us squarely into the preacher's concern. When a religious person cannot separate a theological word from the experience, object, or event the word represents, then we may describe such a person as a literalist or a fundamentalist. In fact, we would do better to say "verbal realist," at least in the theological domain of thinking. When you have trouble translating theological language into the language of experience, when you cannot get the eggs broken, you can suspect that the problem is a form of verbal realism.

Now the main trouble with that is simply that the verbal realist is a prisoner of his or her language. It is probably not overdoing it to say that such people live in worlds of words, and lack the freedom to experience creatively and redemptively either the events of the real world or for that matter the communicative power of language. Langdon Gilkey, for instance, argues quite persuasively that when we lose meaningful God-talk we in time lose touch with the actual experience of transcendence, because we lose the power to hold the experience up linguistically for reflection and interpretation. He believes that when we no longer can "thematize" experience in language, soon the experience itself atrophies and dies.[7]

The theological verbal realist has lost such meaningful theological language just as surely as the rampaging agnostic who does not talk about ultimate things at all. Dr. Wordbinder might be frightened to hear it, but in fact he is close to losing touch with the vitality of his own experience of God's love in Jesus Christ—and his language is the culprit. When he loses the ability to distinguish the word from the thing, he has tragically lost the creative power of both language and experience.

To come back now to the mainstream of the discussion, the verbal realist has lost the appropriate connectedness between the language of preaching and the experience we want to shape. The connections made tend to be from language *to more language,* as witness the preacher who is asked what "trusting the love of Jesus Christ" *means* experientially and replies that it means something like "depending on the grace of God"—connecting language with more language, but not with live experience.

What good is theological language, then? Surely there is some appropriate connection to make between theological language and the experience shaped by communication. Should we stop using God-talk in preaching? Well, yes and no. To the Dr. Wordbinders of the world, it might be best to say yes, stop using God-talk, at least until you rediscover what the appropriate use of such language is. The verbal realism of either the abstractionist or the literalist is one main barrier to redemptive religious experience, certainly through preaching. The two chief offenders who come to mind on that score are at what you might normally think of as opposite ends of the field—the abstruse theological professors and the evangelistic preachers (who are equally abstract in their own ways, though they usually would be the first to deny it. There is nothing "concrete" or even very human about theological formulas and uninterpreted Bible quoting.) To the Dr. Wordbinders, we would be tempted to suggest a moratorium on talking directly about God until they have learned both the power and the limitations of talking, period.

But to the rest of us there is something more to be said, which takes us to the other concept we need for discussing the languages of preaching: context.

Chapter 12. **The Languages of Preaching. II: The Unfolding Context**

For our purposes, *context* is defined as the ordinary understanding of the word, with one added ingredient: the context of language in preaching is the experiential "story" *unfolding in the mind of the listener* in terms of which the language makes sense. The added ingredient of that definition is the "unfolding in the mind of the listener" part, which means simply that for preaching to be adequately "in context," it must become part of "my story," as a listener would put it.

It is not unusual to think of sermons as telling a story—the story of redemption, the story of the Bible, the story of Christian faith, the story of God's love in Jesus Christ, and so on. We are just taking that a step further: the context of language in preaching, from the listener's perspective, is always *my* story, no matter how flawed or fragmented, even if it is my story of redemption, my story of the Bible, my story of Christian faith, my story of God's love in Jesus Christ.

When a message begins, a kind of mental search mission starts in the minds of hearers. From their vast internal computers of stored experience comes a set of meanings, images, and previous understandings to which the unfamiliar incoming message is referred for translation, so to speak. That is the "story," like the accompaniment roll of a player piano, or a film clip backing up the commentary of the evening television news. As soon as that happens, which as a rule takes something like a billionth of a second, communication has become essentially a receiver phenomenon. The meaning of the message is not "transmitted," as we sometimes mistakenly say; it is, so to speak, "transgenerated" in the awareness of the hearer, reassembled in the context of his or her own story.[1]

My three-year-old son is again a good illustration. At that age, this highly verbal little person developed a rather fantastic sense of his own history. Every time he was told something about what was happening, or what something meant, or what someone else had said—the usual daily agenda of conversation with the under-four-feet set—the child would instantly reply by saying, "Whan *I* was a little boy, I would. . . ." and then replay whatever it was that had just been told him. If we said to him, "Look at that Dalmatian dog over there in the fire station," he would reply without missing a beat, "When I was a little boy, I had a Dalmatian dog and he. . . ." at which point we would be off on a fictionalized autobiographical tour that could go on interminably.

What was happening? The three-year-old was not making up something. It never occurred to him to make a distinction between actual, historical report and clever fantasy—they were all the same. The reason they were all the same was quite simply that he was taking in what we told him and transforming it into *his story,* no matter how far-fetched that seemed to the adult mind. To him, it made perfect sense; it was a good way of appropriating information in terms of his own existence. The instant-replay autobiography was a way of making sense of our adult language by weaving it into an experiential story unfolding in his own mind. It was a way of giving language a *context,* without which it would not make three-year-old sense.

As we become adult, we become a good deal more sophisticated. We develop senses of time, reversibility, factuality, and so forth; but in a way we never stop what the three-year-old was so obviously doing: making sense of language by translating it into his unfolding story of existence. If the incoming communication does not easily fit the unfolding story, we will try our hardest to make it fit, even to the extent of completely reversing the speaker's intended significance. If all else fails, we will sometimes abandon the effort altogether and stop listening.

Usually what happens with communication is somewhere in between. The incoming message is partly *appropriated* into our unfolding stories, with or without distortion, and our stories themselves partly *accommodate* themselves to the incoming message.[2] When the experience is over, neither the message nor our inner story is quite what it started out to be, and in that interplay is the dynamic of the communication process.

Communication breaks down when language is decontextualized, when it no longer makes sense to the unfolding inner story that the listener uses as a mental stage on which the words heard are actors. To illustrate, suppose we ask a group of normal human beings to take a little word test. We give them a list of words—*paper, ink,* and *pen*—and ask them to define the last one. They will reply, most likely, by saying that a pen is a writing instrument, or words to that effect. If we give them another list of words—*cattle, barn,* and *pen*—and again ask them to define the last (in context of the list) they will most likely reply that a pen is an enclosure for cattle, or something like that. We can do the same thing, mixing up the lists, with hundreds of normal people, and the results will be generally the same, as everyone would expect. The context established by the first two words determines the meaning of the third in that communication instance.

But suppose we give the same test to an emotionally disturbed person whose illness leads us to diagnose him or her as "schizophrenic." Strangely enough, with a schizophrenic person there is no telling what the response will be. The word *pen,* meaning "writing instrument," may be related to the *cattle–barn* sequence as often as it is to the *paper–ink* list, and vice versa. That finding has led researchers to conclude that schizophrenic patients are characteristically unresponsive to the context of their own and others' speech.[3] Language for them has been decontextualized, and they are unable to relate it to an unfolding inner story in order to make sense of it.

Listen now to a quotation about communication from the listener's point of view:

When people talk to me, it's like a different kind of language. It's too much to hold at once. My head is overloaded, and I can't understand what they say. It makes you forget what you've just heard because you can't get hearing it long enough. It's all in different bits which you have put together again in your head.[4]

Those words might easily be the reaction of a lot of people to a lot of preaching, with its theological jargon, its heaviness, and its abstraction from ongoing experience. In fact, however, the quotation is from a schizophrenic patient describing what it feels like when people talk to him.

All of which leads to the conclusion: when the language of preaching cannot be contextualized and made into "my story," it becomes as meaningless and disorganized to a listener as ordinary speech does to a schizophrenic. Schizophrenic preaching? Perhaps we should not go quite that far, but the connection with psychopathology does underscore the need for awareness of linguistic context in preaching—the need for preaching to be the unfolding story of our deepest yearning and experience of redemption, told chapter by chapter so that it becomes in every true and saving sense "our story."

We preachers may often be guilty of a failure of nerve when it comes to putting sermons together. On the one hand, we profess to believe in the sacramental work of God, bringing the whole of creation into the arena of redemption, *starting* with the ordinary, nonreligious phenomena of human experience. God became human in Jesus Christ to make that point: the drama of salvation goes on in the marketplace, not the temple. But when we begin to preach we do not quite trust our theology. We try to make the work of God start, so far as communication is concerned, with religious things, theological topics, biblical passages, church experiences, religious language, and articles of faith.

God chose to work in the context of our human stories; preachers have a way of turning the tables, as though they were trying to turn human experience into theology rather than to show God's love penetrating human experience. The result is that we decontextualize our language—or worse, we force our hearers to decontextualize it (perhaps out of respect for poor Dr. Wordbinder, who is such a decent fellow even if he doesn't say anything recognizably human in the pulpit). That is not only bad communication, it is bad theology. That "the Word became flesh and dwelt among us" ought to be the most damning indictment of theological verbal realism.

We are now in a position, however, to suggest at least one way in which theological language—whose misuse these chapters have criticized so heavily—does find an appropriate role as one of the languages of preaching. If theological language is not a way of *telling* the story of our experience, it may on the other hand be a way of *reflecting on* that story. It may be a way of giving our own story a family relationship with the similar stories of other people of faith past and present. To use Gilkey's idea, theological language may be a way of identifying and preserving the "theme" of our religious experience.[5]

Imagine two different preachers whose sermons are on the subject of grace. One preacher constructs the sermon along the lines of "Grace is something-or-other," and tries to say what grace is, how it operates in our lives, and what we should do to respond to it. The second preacher takes a much different approach. He does not mention "grace" initially, or at least feels under no compulsion to do so. The sermon does talk about certain aspects of human experience in which we find ourselves the recipients of unexpected reprieves, so to speak, which are gifts of life. The Bible is full of such experiences, and the sermon may focus on one or more of them. The preacher speaks quite ordinarily, talks about human feelings, about our bafflement at being treated better both by other people and by circumstances than we suspect we had coming to us. As the sermon goes along, I, the listener, translate it in terms of my own version of the events being talked about. What the second preacher says is "my story." "Grace" need not yet have been mentioned.

Shortly the preacher is saying that our stories seem to take an odd twist. They grow more intense, more puzzling, our experience is more awesome in its influence on still other aspects of our lives. How are we to make sense of it? Has anyone else been in the same boat? Where does it lead us? Our second preacher nears the end, and begins to say in one way or another, "What we have been talking about and feeling cries out for a name. It has not been an ordinary, take-it-or-leave-it-kind of thing we have been sharing together, and neither will we call it by an ordinary word. We have in our own ways shared the mystery of what Christians through the ages have called the "grace of God in Jesus Christ.""

To be sure, that is an artificial illustration, and no preacher would sound just like that. But see how differently the theological language is used by those two preachers. The first has almost been afraid of losing God's grace if the sermon did not talk directly and theologically about it—the agony of a verbal realist imprisoned in language. The second has told a story, faithful to all the personal depth and ambiguity and intensity of the experience, and then given it all a "theme," a title, so to speak, with the language of theology. Not, you see, "Grace *is* this or that," but "That which we have touched and known is what we call *grace.*" *The second preacher's theology, like Jesus' if we believe the New Testament, is retrospective and interpretative.*

The second preacher had both the connections and the context of language straight; could assume the listener's perspective and talk in a way that connected with the experience he or she was trying to shape in the communication. There were no missing links in the speaking: you did not have to know the secret code already to hear. The preacher was not afraid to break the eggs of theological language in order for the experience for which theology is no more than shorthand to come alive.

The preacher understood what context was about. The sermon's language had to perform on the stage set of its listeners' life stories. Each one was saying inwardly, consciously or unconsciously, "When I was a little kid, I had a Dalmatian dog. . . ."

and the preacher knew it. The communication shaped an experience appropriating the grace of God, because its language was interwoven with the reality of it. As for Zacchaeus, who would take nothing for granted about his position in life, or in trees, for that kind of preacher a kind of salvation comes to our house—the joy of participating in the experience of new life and hope that faithful preaching always promises.

Chapter 13. **Diagnosis: The Missing Step**

The term *diagnosis* is sometimes on the bad-word list of homiletics.[1] Its negative status seems to come from a period of recent history when preachers (and more especially teachers of preaching) were rather touchy about the charge of sermonic irrelevance, and felt themselves duty-bound to prove that preaching *mattered*. Hence the notion that stopping at a statement of what might be awry with things in the human or worldly picture—a diagnosis in other words—was not enough. The pulpit was responsible for cure as well.

In context, that was an appropriate caveat. It is awfully easy, after all, to preach impassioned sermons about what is wrong with life and then retire comfortably to one's study without doing anything about it. Putting that down as inadequate preaching fits in well with a deep running stream of American secular piety that felt—and still feels—that if you cannot make a positive contribution about something you ought to keep your mouth shut. "If you can't say something good, don't say anything at all" is basic American theology that most of us absorbed along with our first solid food. The gadfly has never been a popular or well-tolerated figure on these shores, no matter how perceptive he or she might be. "Diagnosis" in preaching fell victim to the same value: if you could not help things out, keep quiet and make way for those who could.

Unfortunately, we probably threw the baby out with the bathwater. There is, after all, a long and serious biblical tradition of prophecy whose business is not foretelling the future but pointing to hidden flaws in the present, rather like the all-but-invisible hairline metal cracks that when they open cause giant airplanes to fall suddenly from the sky. The idea of this chapter, then, is the double notion that (1) preaching and what we call *diagnosis* belong inseparably together and always have, but that (2) on the whole ministers today are lamentably ill-trained and underskilled as diagnosticians. Toward the end, I want also to suggest a step or two we in theological education might take to create better diagnosticians in preaching and in ministry in general.

Our first task is to get through the linguistic briarpatch of a definition for *diagnosis* and *diagnostician,* which are already tainted words for preachers. The very idea has a medical flavor that many of us would not immediately associate with ministry in any general way, except perhaps in the sphere of pastoral care and counseling. If, however, we focus for a moment on the *gnosis* part, noting that in its native setting the word referred to a kind of everyday, existential *knowing* of something, we begin to make headway. The *dia* simply gives the term penetration and breadth. Diagnosis is a process of coming to know something through and through, so that one can get hold of it better for whatever purposes one has in mind (setting it straight, for instance). My auto mechanic knows my stalling engine differently from the way I do. *I* know that the darned thing keeps cutting out despite my best intentions; *he* knows, on investigation, that a piece of dirt broke loose and lodged in the carburetor during the last tune-up. Here the mechanic is a diagnostician; I am not. If he comes to me for counseling because he feels depressed and detached from life all the time, and

I help ascertain that he is still grieving unsuccessfully over a death that occurred five years ago, our diagnostic roles are reversed. It is a matter, let us say, of the *thoroughness* and *selectiveness* of one's knowing. The diagnostician in whatever phenomenon or task is thorough and selective in a different way from other people, partly because of different perspectives he or she may have on an issue, partly because of training and experience, and partly because of the resources available to be applied to the situation.

That does not begin to exhaust the matter, but it will get us going with a premise: *insofar as Christian theology has always had as one of its root concerns the business of perceiving life extraordinarily* (from the perspective of the life, death, and resurrection of Jesus Christ), *and then nurturing different behavior on the basis of that different perception, then it has had a diagnostic agenda from the beginning.* Whether we think of the prophets, the deliberate shifting of perception wrought by the parables, the "You have heard it said, but I say...." stance of Jesus, the "Repent and believe" challenge to everydayness of the earliest church, or the more dramatic examples of apocalyptic, the diagnostic theme has been central. It is more than just gnostic, more than merely contemplative or fascinative or even pragmatic knowing that Christian theology has meant. It has been a knowing that is more thorough and more selective, in service to but distinct from the "divine imperative" that has been Christianity's traditional motive power. Preaching, of all the activities of the church, has always been charged with a special responsibility for cultivating that kind of *knowing.*

You could say, then, that preachers are called to be diagnosticians in the classic sense of the term. The question is not so much *whether* we ought to be in that role, but rather how adequate we have been. Three kinds of information that are increasing in volume suggest that we need to take very seriously a failure of diagnostic competence among ministers and then to ask whether that itself suggests some needed changes in theological thinking and education.

The first source of information is the phenomenal increase of conservative religious activity and its administrative off-shoot, the so-called church growth movement. I discover that practically no one in today's master of divinity student generation has ever heard of Dean Kelley's *Why Conservative Churches Are Growing*.[2] Evidently that was a manifesto whose half-life was shorter than, in my opinion at least, it deserved. Kelley's main thesis almost got lost in the shouting that followed, but it is essentially a point about diagnosis. He argued that while liberal theology was busy endorsing everyone's creativity, freedom, responsibility, and potentially, conservative religion and especially conservative preaching were providing *meaning systems* for people's lives. Conservative religion was, although Kelley does not use the word, that I recall, performing a diagnostic function: telling people that it knew them more thoroughly (in terms of what "really mattered" to them) and more selectively (in terms of where the difficulties they experienced "really" lay) than anyone or anything else. Given that people and societies are hurting, it is all too easy for us to write off the conservative palliation in disgust as cheap grace, an answer system, or authoritarian dominance. That may be, but whatever else we call it the conservative response to people's frustration, sense of meaninglessness, and impotence was and is diagnosis that allows its recipients to believe that they have because of it a better chance of healing; that is, access to whatever it takes to make things better.

We ought to rest very uneasily with the cynical notion that people do not really want to know what is wrong with them and therefore flock to leaders who give easy, painless answers. The evidence simply does not support it. Discounting boredom, there is probably more emotional and social discomfort evoked in conservative religious observance than in any of our mainline churches. The differentiating factor is the presence or absence of a sense on the part of mainline church constituencies that they are thoroughly and selectively *known* by people who can help them. I happen to think the diagnoses that appear in conservative circles are often wrong; but that is a matter of quality and content, not process itself. For mainline religion to cut off the process because of a quarrel with the content is cutting off the nose to spite the face.

The hidden agenda of Kelley's book, by the way, was that there is no reason why more liberal theological premises cannot *also* function to give life meaning and value. The diagnostic capability is not vested intrinsically with one theological position or another, and we lose track of that at our peril. The rise of fringe conservatism in theology suggests a decline in diagnostic sensitivity and usefulness among other more central theological positions.

(Here, by the way, is opportunity for one of the few exercises in prediction this book indulges in, but one that strikes me as terribly important. We now have in this country a very large number of people, mostly young, who either are or will someday soon be *former* conservatives in religious practice. They will constitute a group of people with very special needs for pastoral theological help when the religious systems that have sustained them in adolescence and young adulthood themselves wear thin and let them down. How will we help them come to terms with their disillusionment? How will we help them understand what happened to them and why? That is a diagnostic ministry par excellence, and it will come to preaching first. I worry very seriously whether we will be up to the task, which I suspect is going to be more formidable than any of us now realize. It is ironic that one signal of the importance of diagnosis in ministry may also turn out to create one of the greatest needs for it.)

A second source of information about diagnostic failure is more diffuse but at the same time more familiar: the commonplace stereotypes and "cartoon images" of what ministers and ministry are like. We do not need to be extensively reminded of the traditional picture of the parson as a pious old windbag who has an answer (usually ridiculous) for everything and a solution for nothing. In a less bombastic vein, pastoral counselors tell us they are saddened over and over again when people flinch ever so slightly on learning that they are ministers. When they speak to counselees about that and about the increasing number of ministers who have had some training in profes- sional helping skills, people are invariably surprised. "I didn't realize ministers could do that" is the theme of the response, almost universally. The underlying point is that it has seldom occurred to people to look to their ministers as diagnosticians. Quite to the contrary, the stereotype is that the minister is called in to put the pieces together (or bury them) after the diagnosticians of society—doctors, lawyers, social workers, and the like—have done their work. For that matter, how often does it occur to *us* that diagnosis is part of our pastoral and theologi- cal task from the beginning, and that a primary locus of that responsibility is in preaching.[3]

Theological writing itself has been hard on diagnosis. In homiletics, as we have seen, the very idea of diagnosis has been a whipping boy for several generations, students being warned that too much diagnosis in their sermons (presumably at the expense of "proclamation") is a bad thing. Strangely though, in the sermons I hear (which amount sometimes to several a week, mostly from students) the almost universal weakness is a failure to think diagnostically about a biblical text, a human situation, a theological idea, or a social relationship. I have taken to recommending my beloved mystery and spy novels as the most essential preparation a student preacher can do these days; at least they let one kibbitz on diagnosis par excellence!

The domain of seminary experience leads to the third source of information underlying the thesis of this chapter. In Doctor of Ministry seminar work, where candidates are asked to ana- lyze, interpret theologically and behaviorally, and intervene in troublesome ministry situations, the commonest finding is that they cannot think diagnostically. One example will illustrate.

The qualifying examination given to Doctor of Ministry can- didates at one seminary consists of brief case studies, all based on real-life experiences of ministry that the students are to analyze, critique, and propose a course of action for. In one question, the following situation was given. A young couple have been married for eight months. The wife is finishing a master's degree in special education, and the husband is a registered pharmacist. The pastor in the case had not been asked to marry the couple eight months previously because the wife's parents thought him "too liberal" even though the wife was a member of the pastor's church. In the case as given, the couple have come to talk to the pastor because they have just discovered that the wife is pregnant, against their wishes, and they have all but decided that she should have an abortion. Their purpose in coming to the pastor, as they say, is to ask God's forgiveness if they do in fact go ahead with the abortion. The question contained a few more details, but that is the basic situation. The issue in part posed for Doctor of Ministry candidates taking the exam was, "If you were in the pastor's shoes, what would you attempt to do in relation to the couple's dilemma and on what grounds, theologically, would your efforts be based?"

Readers of the completed examinations were dismayed to find that almost without exception the answers from well-qualified ministers took the following shape: the couple was "affirmed" in their dilemma; it was pointed out that the Bible was basically silent on the abortion issue, and therefore no guidance was to be had from that source; the pastor was willing to "work through" the question with the couple if they wished; most answers sympathized with the couple as being caught in a web of unfortunate circumstances; in virtually every case the couple themselves were cast in an entirely positive, nonreactive, perhaps victimized, and wholly innocent light.

There was no attempt in these answers to reach a diagnosis of the situation as presented in terms of psychodynamics, theological and ethical issues and decisions, the nature of religious participation and faith, or underlying factors that might possibly be influential. Missed entirely, though quite apparent in the language of the exam question itself, were such factors as these: the couple could be seen as an anxious pair with rigid "early

married" plans, who now sought (perhaps unwittingly) to box
the minister into a corner with something like "preforgive-
ness"; the dominant concern presented was their own comfort,
with no mention whatever of any responsibility for the potential
child or anyone else; the educational and professional level of
both husband and wife could virtually rule out the "accident"
possibility, certainly in psychodynamic terms, of the pregnancy.
In other words, so far as diagnostic acumen was concerned, the
couple was let off scot-free of any form of responsibility either
past or future, the entire Christian tradition of ethical decision
making was ignored, and the theological substratum of the
entire response was a deistic picture of a God who "affirms" but
does not guide, either directly, through the witness of the
church, or the ministry of a pastor, any human decision or
analysis. What we saw in these answers was a massive failure of
"thorough and selective knowing."

The list of instances goes into the thousands, and when they
reach the pulpit they have a haunting familiarity. What appears
is a rush to premature *therapeia* based on no evident diagnostic
hypotheses. Ministers apparently do not think diagnostically;
they are reluctant to assess negative factors in either situations
or motivational patterns; they are alarmingly limited to "affirming" persons, "facilitating" (but not speaking directly about)
decisions, and "representing" (but not interpreting) the Christian tradition. Now there is nothing at all wrong with any of
those things; heaven knows, we need them! But when they are,
in effect, decisions of ministerial tactic or strategy without
previous diagnosis of what is really going on and why, they are
as effective and as dangerous as Old Dr. Quack's Cancer Salve,
to remember an aphorism of H. L. Mencken.

Why are we so inept at diagnosis, and what can we do about
it so far as preaching is concerned? The *why* question is vastly
complicated, but for a start three deficiencies in our ministerial
armamentorium need consideration. *First, we ministers lack an
adequate diagnostic language.* A great deal of highly competent
and constructive writing has recently been done on this very

point.[4] Preachers are accused of being ersatz psychotherapists when they use the language of psychodynamics; they are accused of being pietists or worse when they speak of *sin, forgiveness, grace,* or use any of the usual theological terms. If they talk about social and community dynamics, they are accused of being amateur sociologists. If they lapse into the imagery of story or fable, they are written off as woolly-headed and romantic.

Part of the problem here is that we have not taken seriously enough the difference between theological conceptualization (as, for instance, in doctrinal theology) on the one hand, and articulation of extraordinary experience on the other, so far as the difference affects and generates the language of our profession. To be a bit ironic about it, we have not adequately diagnosed the bankruptcy of the language system of Christian reflection in a highly complex and stubborn secular age, as adequate to the diagnostic dimension of ministry. That has been a concern in several of these chapters, especially the last two, and it is pivotal here.

It can be argued that once the distinction (and to be sure, the interaction) between language of experience and language of interpretation or conceptualization is made, then *it may not matter* so much whether our diagnostic speech is taken from the lexicon of psychiatry, theology, systems theory, or whatnot, depending on the milieu of the participants. It is the *confusion* of those two levels of intention in speaking that causes trouble diagnostically, rather than the selection of one or another vocabulary per se.

A second factor appears to be an endemic intolerance among preachers for ambiguity, uncertainty, and intractability in the soul-searing situations they encounter every day of their pastoral lives. That, too, we have encountered before in these pages, and now it comes home to roost. Ministers seem to want to see themselves as "fix-up" people who can put things right; the frustration of having to diagnose a situation in which there is *nothing* we can do may have soured us on the entire diagnostic enterprise. We will take a chance on affirming, facilitating, and representing in the absence of thorough and selective knowing, in the pathetic hope it might do some good and keep us from despair. To use Seward Hiltner's terms, we have let ourselves think of theology as an answer system (and ourselves as answer people) rather than as a descriptive and interpretative system (and ourselves as descriptive and interpretative—in sum, diagnostic—people). One cannot but think that a resistance to diagnosis is also a resistance to the bottom-line condition in which we find ourselves: disciples of Jesus Christ who, try as we will, cannot quite bring it off the way God does.

Thirdly, we have to suspect that a contributing factor to diagnostic failure is our loss of any appropriate theological sense of judgment and what it means in the daily comings and goings of human existence. We have emerged within the last generation or two from an era of ministry that was rightly put down for its authoritarian, judgmental, and intolerant attitudes. No one wants to go back, partly because we see how off-base it was, and partly because as often as not we were just embarrassingly (and sometimes smugly) wrong. Perhaps we went overboard. For fear of returning to that pattern of ministry, we now avoid anything that looks like "judgment," including appropriate diagnostic judgments that are the minister's Christian heritage. I recall with horror the way the "Judge not that you be not judged" command was drummed into my consciousness as a young person. Judging was sinful, period. I now realize not with horror but with sadness that no one made the equally plausible construction of that text and idea: "judgment" is a risk on the part of the one who makes it, often necessary for the sake of another person, but never exempting our own investment. It is an offer of shared responsibility for someone's or something's future, and an invitation to mobilize one's resources, confess one's sins, and trust the incarnate work of God. All of which, I would now say, is what diagnosis means. To "judge"—without a back-up answer in your hip pocket, without any realistic hope of fixing up what you have just identified, and without protection, comfort, or happiness from the task that has gripped you —may be the ingress of grace. Preaching needs at least to take that possibility more seriously than it has in the past.

  · What can we do about that, especially if we are long out of seminary and living educationally on pitifully inadequate "continuing education allowances" that at best allow travel to one short seminar or the purchase of a dozen or fewer books and tapes each year? Well, for a starter we can pay more attention to the kind and amount of the "preacher's education," which is in quotation marks because so much of it seems to go on in circumstances that do not appear educational—like emergency rooms, cocktail lounges, waiting in line to have your car inspected, and the like. I have three fairly outrageous suggestions to make.

  First, we can boycott all seminars, courses, or books that purport to teach ministers how to heal, treat, administer, counsel, proclaim, or otherwise fix up *until* we have a prior attention to critical interpretation and diagnosis in theological and secular perspectives. Preachers can be more selective in their educational shopping; they can start asking for help with diagnosis even when the wares most prominently displayed in the marketplace are of the fix-up, how-to, you-can-be-more-effective variety. The uninitiated may not realize that seminaries, publishers, and other purveyors of knowledge (such as book authors) are as subject to the influence of supply and demand as any other marketplace. By and large, we will give you what you ask for. The most critically important seminar course ever imagined will not last three semesters if no more than a handful of students elect to take it. The interest among some clergy, for example, in Doctor of Ministry study that aims for critical, integrative analysis of ministry situations is encouraging; but it is more than overbalanced, I am afraid, by the steady demand for "practical" improvement offerings with nary a stray thought for the diagnostic function or dimension of preaching.

  That brings up the second outrageous suggestion. We can make sure that at least half of the preacher's ongoing educational experience involves analysis of some form of situational, case-oriented presentations in which diagnosis of our own work is the first step toward effective and theologically responsible preaching. That is tougher than it sounds. We preachers are notoriously shy about letting other preachers have a look at our sermons. I once participated in a "cluster" of pastors who convened weekly for shared biblical study and sermon preparation on common texts. The next logical step seemed to be for the group to discuss the sermons that came out of the group study, right? Wrong. With rare backpeddling grace, the group unanimously (with my exception) elected to bypass the diagnostic approach to their own sermons. Until we learn to receive diagnosis and participate in it, we shall never learn how to do it.

That resistance notwithstanding, though, these days the idea of situational analysis of actual ministry, especially preaching, will be much less controversial than it would have been, say, ten years ago. Keep in mind that the purpose of this situation-oriented theological education is not to make theological concepts or traditional data go down more smoothly, but rather to expose the vital, experiential foundation of the whole theological enterprise, with its footings in the diagnosis that biblical writers had in mind when they enjoined us to have the "mind of Christ."

Third, at risk of not being taken as seriously as I intend, we should see that our daily reading includes generous helpings of the great literary genre of intrigue and criticism, be it in the form of mystery novel, psychiatric case study, civil law, nuclear physics, or the essays of E. B. White. That will achieve two ends: the cultivation of diagnostic acumen, and the discovery that language of any kind is fused with reality only at our peril. It is discouraging to hear preachers relegate their Agatha Christie or Robert Ludlum to the category of after-hours "pleasure" (which it surely is) rather than prime-time sermon preparation (which it surely should be). Equally depressing are the book displays laid out traditionally at judicatory gatherings, continuing education extravaganzas, and the like. They are almost all meaty and theological, which is fine, and almost never include criticism and intrigue, which are the prime arenas these days for observing keen diagnosis at work.

These suggestions are not a panacea, of course; they are intended to stir some thinking we might not have done before about learning to become better diagnosticians. I firmly believe that we preachers will be grateful to discover that our pulpit work has all along had a potential significance that is in some ways both more modest and more crucial than we have let ourselves imagine. Recovering that through diagnosis just might prove to be the alternative to the homiletical malaise in which all too many otherwise perceptive and gifted preachers find themselves.

IV
LIVING IN THE BLUEPRINT
The Receiving End of Preaching

We have no trouble saying theologically that sometimes being willing to lose something is the only way to find it—be it the life Jesus spoke of or something lower in magnitude. We are conscious of the dangers of holding too tightly to something, and of the liberation that comes when we let go enough for it to regain its shape and meaning. Communication in preaching can be thought of that way. The point is focused in a dictum that has appeared before in these pages, but is now the organizing motif for the coming section: *communication is a receiver phenomenon.* There is always a gap, a discontinuity, between our own thinking and intentions, and the experience on the receiving end where communication, if it occurs at all, ultimately happens. Fortunately, or perhaps miraculously all things considered, that gap is bridged often enough for us to become fairly sanguine about the communication process itself. Only in the breakdowns do its dynamics appear in the bold relief necessary to study them. Day in and day out, we communicate successfully and effortlessly. When something goes amiss, we begin to see that no amount of tinkering with the source of messages does any good except with self-conscious reference

to their destination: the receiver. Looking at things from that
perspective is our business now.

Chapter 14. **Sharing the Study**

If we were honest with ourselves, chances are we would someday notice a discrepancy between the "finishes" of our sermons
and of our own faiths, the sermons coming out a good deal
more polished and nice than their authors' own struggles to
be faithful. After all, most of us spent a good bit of time in
seminary and later learning how to be at least competent, if not
eloquent, as wordsmiths. That a sermon might just turn out to
be *too* well crafted is hardly ever a real worry—but it should
be.

The fact is sermons can be too polished, too well-wrought,
too artful. At worst, they may trigger anxiety and resistance as
our friend with his role playing in Chapter 9. More commonly,
though, the danger of an overly polished sermon is not so much
that it will put people off as that it fails to give them one essential thing in the preaching experience: a chance to join a pilgrimage of faith by struggling and growing *along with* the
preacher. That is the main point. If we want our people to grow
in faith through the preaching we do, the most ready-to-hand
tool is our own struggle to preach. Sadly, we too often close our
people out of that experience rather than invite them in. The
classic statement of the role of the person of the preacher in
preaching was made by Phillips Brooks and his dictum of "truth
through personality."[1] What Brooks called for in the 1890s has
been given more contemporary expression through the clinical
pastoral education movement, with its emphasis on congruence, straightforwardness in emotional interaction, and hones-

ty in pastoral relationships. Preaching, though, has sometimes been a slow student. What John Scotford said back in 1927 has a hauntingly familiar sound:

> Homiletic instruction has commonly centered about sermon building.... Such training has commonly produced sermonizers rather than preachers.... Phillips Brooks' definition of preaching as "truth through personality" is commonly accepted, but its implications for homiletic training are rarely acted upon. The writing of sermons is an incidental matter; the training of the personality of the preacher is fundamental.[2]

Only one segment of the broad spectrum of the "person" of the preacher concerns us here, and that is the dynamic of sermon preparation as an integral part of the message itself. Simply put, a lot of what we have to say as preachers is a report, so to speak, on our own struggle to have something to say, our own encounter with a biblical text, our own sense of *faith seeking understanding*. To get a better idea of what is going on here, let us take a look into the study of a hypothetical preacher at work.

He (or she) has done the spadework of preparing a sermon: chosen a text, done a basic exegetical "scan" of it, brainstormed some of his own responses to what the text seems to be saying, even dug a little bit into the original language for a couple of terms that seemed vague to him. The text is still flat. Its semantic meaning is clear now, there are no puzzling bits of syntax or obscure cultural references left dangling. The problem of the text is "out there," it has no feeling of "fit" or importance to anything the preacher can identify today.

He reads the text again, and this time something catches his attention. A clue is given to what kind of person the text originally was addressed to. Point of contact? No, the preacher himself is not like that ancient addressee; we've come a long way since then. Still, something is bothering him, he doesn't know what.

He sets the work aside—a good beginning, time for a break.

In an afternoon of hospital calling, he does not think about his troublesome text; he thinks about the pain he tries to comfort, the uncertainty he tries to reassure in the people he has seen. What a gift to be able to walk away from the hospital, there but for the grace of God. . . . Or is it a little bit of "Thank God I'm not like that!"? No matter. Other duties, family time, back eventually to the thin sermon preparation folder.

This time for some reason the text is not flat at all; it has become troublesome. What is it? The preacher tries an interpretation, carries an idea through several stages. Yes, it makes sense. No, it doesn't. Give up, that way will not work. Here is something else odd, a detail he missed before. What was it about yesterday afternoon at the hospital that rings a bell? It is hard, it just will not come! This way and that the preacher comes and goes in and out of the text. Fragments of recognition of himself fall into place. Ideas are tried and given up. Flashes of other people come into view, the pastoral work of the week, a recollection from last year, a phrase of song from the radio.

The preacher realizes the text is trying to address a part of him he does not much want to know about—the dark underside of faith, the doubt, the meanness, the easy settling for second best and home before dark. He struggles to avoid it; cannot; tries to bargain a little with its meaning, loses; turns his back on it for something more hopeful, is stuck with it. The preacher gives in; a slim ray of light falls into one of the shadowy areas of his understanding, and the text is suddenly no longer flat, but three-dimensional, alive, ready to preach.

And what now shall he preach? Most of us know that most of us in that preacher's shoes would simply and confidently preach the end product of all that preparation. We would share with our congregation what is essentially the conclusion of our own struggling, and in so doing we would be radically shortchanging both them and ourselves, by mistakenly thinking that the end product of our preparation will be of some use to them without their own participation in a similar struggle to understand and grow. Should it be such a surprise to us when what seemed so important back in the study gets so little response on Sunday morning no matter how artful our sermon crafting— possibly *because* of our polish?

The point here is a straightforward plea for preachers to let people into their studies, so to speak, *so that the process of developing a sermon at times comes close to being the sermon itself.* It is an attempt to take seriously in the area of preaching what is already a commonplace in Christian education, for instance: that the best learning happens when people discover something for themselves, and the best teaching is guiding people through a search process rather than handing them the end product neatly packaged for portability. What the preacher fundamentally has to say emerges from his or her wrestling in preparation, and the end product will never be fully intelligible apart from its developmental history in the life of its author. Its context is a struggle to understand and be faithful—as much for the receiver as for the preacher. That is the linchpin of the whole business. The message of preaching is a process rather than an outcome; an invitation *to* rather than an explanation *of,* a story in the making as much as a history of the past. When we were kids doing junior high arithmetic homework, the teacher always wanted to see our calculations as well as the final answers; knowing how to get there was the main thing. Things have not changed much.

Keep in mind that we are talking about a dynamic process now, not any particular style of sermon. Sometimes a preacher may want to construct a sermon as a kind of guided tour through the preparation process—a "diary of a sermon," it could be called. More often a preacher will probably structure the sermon in ways that allow people to contribute their own situations and experiences to the unfolding of the preparation. Whatever style is chosen, the mortal enemy of the whole discovery process is the overcrafted sermon that asks to be contemplated and admired but not joined. And whatever style is chosen, the sermon that is honest about what it does not know and cannot straighten out, as well as what it has come to in faith, is more inviting to the life of faith than the one that hedges its bets behind a show of false certainty, no matter how artful.

Chapter 15. **The Work of the Kitchen: Digestion**

Once a pastor had to make a trip to a town half a day's drive away, and one of his parishioners asked if she might ride along, since she too had business there. The pastor was agreeable, and on the ride the woman was gracious enough to say how much she had gotten out of the pastor's sermons. In particular, she said the sermon two weeks ago was very helpful to her because she "found" herself in it just at a time she needed to. The pastor stared uncomfortably at the road ahead as the woman talked on. He nodded appreciatively at her words, but inside he experienced a hidden turmoil: try as he would, he could not remember for the life of him what he had said that Sunday!

The story is true, as I should know, and the moral intends no ingratitude to the woman. But what we should hope is not that people remember our sermons but rather that they should digest them. To some preachers, that may come as a relief. We have spent a lot of effort trying to coin the memorable phrase, to simplify the organization of a sermon for easy recollection, even producing mimeographed copies of our weekly efforts lest people forget them. How unrealistic we have been, and with perfectly straight faces at that! *We* cannot possibly remember all our own sermons; why should we expect other people to perform such a herculean feat?

More than that, even: is it possible not only that remembering sermons is too much to ask, but positively detrimental to what we intend? We come face to face here with the difficult, near-bottom-line question of what we aim to accomplish in preaching anyway. The answer is going to be somewhat different for each of us, but I daresay that deep down we would get near-consensus on this much: we hope that preaching cultivates a growth process in our people so that in whatever mysterious ways they come closer to the presence and will of God in their lives. In short, we want the sermon to be used in that process more than we want it be admired from afar. We want our sermons digested rather than remembered, and that is as it should be. We want them to enter the whole nurturing process and that, confessedly, means that we see our best efforts used up, forgotten for what they were when preached in order to become something vital when lived—as the most elegant cuisine loses its outside beauty when it enters the inner chemistry of nutrition.

I look in my backyard at a priceless legacy from previous owners: a giant compost heap, rich, black, and crumbly, with the clean, dew-fresh smell of the forest floor. What a pity, I say to myself, to have to turn that into the garden's heavy clay! I will not see the compost next year; my fierce gardener's pride will have to switch from the black gold of the compost heap to the red juiciness of fresh tomatoes that it nurtured. The original wealth is there all right, doing what it is supposed to do under the soil's surface; it has become part of the growth process.

If Barth is right that the proclamation of the Word in preaching is a part of the very revelation of Jesus Christ and the scriptures, then it is a serious theological mistake for us to think of sermons mechanistically as rhetoric or speech or any such thing.[1] If our christology is often based on the Philippians' hymn celebrating Christ's emptying himself for humankind (Phil. 2:1–11), then why should we balk so when it comes time to empty our sermons into the lives of those who consume them? Surely the idea of a grain of wheat falling to the ground and dying is not wholly foreign to preaching itself. A preacher who had been at it for going on twenty-five years was once asked why he worked so hard these days preparing sermons. After all, did he not have several hundred, at a conservative guess, in the barrel? No, he replied, I never kept my notes or files. Maybe I could dredge up a half dozen or so from a running notebook I keep, but the rest are gone.

Think of it: there is not likely to be more than a handful of that lifetime's worth of sermons that are remembered by an occasional person here and there. Mostly they are gone: digested, not remembered. To most of us, there is something professionally horrifying about that story—to those of us, for instance, who take photocopies of our collected sermon outlines when we move, lest the moving van and its precious cargo dive over a cliff along the way. But there is something faithful there, too, for which most of us could stand to reach. It works its way back into the preacher's study, where more often than we want to admit we work as though we were aiming for our sermon to be remembered through the ages, rather than used up in the lifeblood of those who hear it.

Think what differences in our preparation it might make to think of sermons being digested rather than remembered. We might, for instance, spend more time clarifying just what we want a particular sermon to accomplish, what nutrient we want it to be in the growth process. We might worry less about having a zingy introduction and a heart-stopping conclusion, concentrating instead on the real drama of lives changing and hearts opening in mundane congregational ways. We might be more suspicious of theological jargon when we ask not how beautiful it will look but how digestible it will be in understanding. We might be willing to cover less territory in any one sermon, but do it more thoroughly and more personally. When a single text could easily provide three sermons, we might resist the temptation to make them three points of one sermon. We might picture more vividly in our minds' eyes the lives of those who will hear the sermons, speaking more directly and personally to their situations. We might be less harried by the need to keep people interested, and more committed to the task of keeping them fed.

Thinking of sermons in this way may also have the effect of drawing more closely together the processes of textual interpretation and pulpit communication. The relationship of hermeneutic and communicative dynamics is another whole subject in itself, but at least this much can be said here: if the

Bible is seen hermeneutically as the attempt of people to articulate the shape and the momentousness of their religious experience so that others might participate in it as though it were their own, then the task of sermon preparation is largely to create a communication environment where the text can do its own preaching, with the preacher as guide and host. A preacher who is after recollection will never be quite as free to trust that invitational process as one who sees the task "digestively," so to speak.

A crucial difference of perspective is at work here. Commonly we think of hermeneutics as having to do with interpreting biblical texts, and indeed that is a primary meaning of the concept. What we should not overlook, however, is that, functionally speaking, the Bible is not only the recipient of hermeneutical attention from interpreters, but is also itself performing a hermeneutic on the experience of both its original participants and modern readers. Preaching is involved with hermeneutics not just to interpret texts, but perhaps more centrally *preaching is involved with the Bible as a hermeneutic on existence.* The biblical text itself, then, is not so much the problematical nut in need of cracking so far as preaching is concerned as it is a major communication source in its own right. There is a real and literal sense in which the text and the preacher are attempting to accomplish the same goals through the same processes, side by side, and should more properly be thought of as yoke mates than sparring partners. The preacher attempts not so much to perform an operation *on* the text as to facilitate the text's own communication with modern hearers. Insofar as the sermon is the preacher's tool for accomplishing such a task, it would be a serious mislocation of importance to enshrine the sermonic tool itself as an object or event to be memorialized.

We are mixing metaphors here—nutrition and carpentry and who knows what else—but the underlying point is crucial enough and overlooked enough to be worth spending some energy on. Another way of saying it would be to remind preachers that while in the heat of battle they may look on their ser-

mons as the fruit and product of their labor, from a communicative and theological slant those same sermons are no more—or
less—than instruments we use to facilitate the growth of our
hearers. Oh, to be sure, there will always be room for a certain
pride of workmanship that we quietly enjoy to ourselves. My
dentist is very proud of the complicated artistry of the porcelain
tooth he fashioned for me, and far be it from me to take away
from his pleasure; but he and I both know that the real importance of what happened has to do with my being able to eat and
smile again thanks to the utility of the dental art. The same
attitude can be both humbling and freeing for preachers.

Chapter 16. **Guided Tours, or How to Listen to a Sermon**

Running as a subtext through the last few chapters has been a
lurking question, something like "How on earth do we get our
people to play ball by the same rules as we use in preaching? If
so much of this process depends on their participation and
their understanding of what is going on, how do we get them
on board, knowledgeably and cooperatively?"

Well, incredible as it may seem, the best answer is that *we
should tell them.* The vast majority of people in our congregations have never in their lives heard a preacher say anything
directly and clearly to them about what is involved in *hearing* a
sermon. Few of us have ever preached a sermon entitled "How
to Listen to a Sermon," in which we spelled out what we hoped
for in preaching, what we asked for in participation from our
people, and what anyone could expect as a result of the whole
process week after week. The damning fact is that we preachers

have talked to our people about everything under heaven *except* how to do the very thing we ask them to do on a weekly basis— listen to and participate in a sermon. The more you think about it, the more incredible it gets.

It would be all right, of course, if preaching were an ordinary kind of communication that we learn how to handle as part of growing up, like school lessons, television dramas, and Daddy's explanations of things. But for preaching we make claims unlike those of any other communication experience, about the revelation of God through human speech, about the meeting of God and humankind in the story of salvation, about the commitment to discipleship through hearing the call of Jesus in modern words, about the work of grace in human lives, about the knowledge of truth that sets us free from bondage. As long as we insist on making such claims as those, we bear the responsibility of teaching people how to participate in a communication environment unique at the very least for the momentousness of its demands, to say nothing of the oddity of its dynamics.

There are at least two primary ways to teach people how to listen to our sermons. The first and most direct is to plan on some regular basis to preach on that very subject—through a "teaching sermon," if you like. It should be a very straightforward statement of what the preacher is aiming for, hoping for, wanting from the congregation. There is no reason why such a sermon should not be an annual event, with different emphases each year as the preacher's own understanding and style grow and change.

A second and more indirect way to cultivate the arcane knowledge of sermon listening is to be especially sure that each individual sermon is clear about its own expectations of its hearers. To understand a bit more fully how that works, we need to talk about two subtle but vital aspects of human communication— *metacommunication* and the *communication contract*.

Metacommunication, like other "meta-" concepts, means simply "communication about communication." We automatically do it all the time when we include in our messages certain instructions, sometimes overt and sometimes implicit, for how we want the receiver of those messages to respond. As my seven-year-old son is turning away from a scolding we both know I am on the verge of giving him, I say with rising anger, "Now *listen* to me, son!" That is a bit of metacommunication. It is not the message I intend, but an instruction about the message that is to come. It asks for a certain level of seriousness and attention; it forewarns the child that what he is about to hear is not, let us say, a bedtime story or a rundown of the Phillies' best season. Along with the words will go a certain tone of voice, an inflection of speech, and perhaps a body gesture or two like a pointing finger or my hands on stubborn little shoulders. All that is metacommunication.

In ordinary conversation, the dozens of phrases, gestures, tones of voice, and body postures we automatically use serve metacommunicative purposes. The concept alone is easy enough to understand, but its work in practice is a highly complex interplay that we *do* naturally, but understand only with great effort. Anyone whose vocation is communication, however, must learn to be aware of metacommunicative behavior even when it is at work automatically without our knowing it. The most common and frequent opportunity for teaching people how to listen to sermons is through constant metacommunication as the process unfolds. When a preacher says, "I want you to listen to this story and see if you recognize yourself in it, despite the different circumstances," that is a formal and explicit bit of metacommunication. When the tone of our voice changes a notch toward the momentous and conclusive, everyone in the church (and especially the organist, who has to move fast now) knows the sermon is nearly over. That is an informal and highly implicit bit of metacommunication, but the same process nevertheless.

The point is that the more direct we are in telling people what we want and expect of them moment by moment, the better our communication is likely to be. If a hard-to-understand point is coming up in a sermon, we can say, "What this leads us to is not

easy to understand, but is worth the effort. Let's take it one step
at a time," thus instructing the people about what level of effort
is required of them, warning them that the price of inattention
is going to be confusion, and reassuring them that somewhere
along the line their labor is going to pay off. It is direct metacommunication.

Obviously one could overdo it, rather like teaching someone
how to eat lobster by saying, "First, grasp the nutcrackers between thumb and forefinger and lift from the table. . . ." On the
whole, though, we preachers are probably much more afraid
than we ought to be of spoiling the effect of our prose with
metacommunication. The strong evidence is that we have un-
derdone it, not the reverse. That is equally true, if not more so,
for communication contracts.

Contracts for communication are more structured parts of a
message that serve the metacommunicative process. In homiletics, we have been calling contracts for communication "introductions" without always knowing just what function and
purpose, from a communicative point of view, that hallowed
feature of every sermon had. From this standpoint, however, an
introduction's purpose is to establish between preacher and
hearers a "contract for communication," a shared agreement
that in the message to follow we will be talking about certain
things in certain ways, trying to get to certain points of understanding or action, and each contributing this or that to the
unfolding process. The idea of a "contract" is familiar enough
in pastoral care and counseling, where it refers to the agreement to work toward certain goals and in certain ways between
care giver and care receiver. It operates the same way in preaching; both are incidents of the same communication phenomenon.

An introduction seen as a contract for communication has a
role to play in the process of communication in preaching far
more than as an aspect of the content of the particular message.
It is not just a smooth way to begin. True, the introduction is
going to have some informational relationship to the "body" of

the message. But it is important to realize that it has a larger purpose, too: setting the contract for communication, coming to an agreement about how we will handle and what we will make of the message content that is to come.

As with most metacommunication, on the whole we probably err in introductions more on the side of subtlety than overdirection. We try to be too clever with our introductions, losing the functional aspect. Or perhaps we plunge right into our preaching work, with nary a thought for getting any agreement with our captive audience on what is about to happen. Be that as it may, whenever the contract is set, the introduction is over. Sometimes that will take one sentence, sometimes half the sermon. The rule is functional rather than rhetorical, just as our understanding of the introduction now is not rhetorical. The communication question to ask is "When has the contract been set?" rather than "How long should the introduction be?" Each sermon will be different, although it is fair to say that congregations learn their preachers' styles just as we preachers do our congregations'. We could rely much more on that than we usually do. Telling a congregation that you are about to start a certain kind of sermon that from past experience everyone knows proceeds in a certain way, is a highly refined and efficient contract setting, which has the clarity and honesty of being up front where we all know what is happening. Preaching three-point sermons every week of the year with no comment on what is happening yields the same sureness of expectation, but if a preacher has been at it for twenty-five minutes and then announces that Point 3 is about to begin, a sigh too deep for words takes hold of the congregation, which is more apt to feel trapped than contracted with.

Perhaps it is time to explode one venerable myth about sermon introductions. Time after time, we have all heard that the purpose of an introduction is "to get people's attention." Now really, when was the last time anyone saw a preacher step into the pulpit at sermon time and *not* have everyone's attention? The rather more painful fact is that we already have their attention and their willingness as a free gift—for a while. What we have is *their offer* to participate in the preaching that is about to happen. We do not need to "get it," but we surely do need to *use* it by establishing a contract for communication. There will hardly ever be a time when the preacher does not start with people's attention; there may be many times indeed when it is completely gone five minutes later, not really because they were not interested so much as because they did not know what was expected—both for them and of them. *That* is what we need to work on.

Two objections are sometimes raised to the whole idea of contracts, metacommunication, and introductions. They need to be taken seriously because in themselves the objections are coming from serious attempts to preach well. One has to do with the discovery process, and the other with language style itself.

The first objection says that often a sermon intends to build to a conclusion in such a way that people join a discovery process along the way, reaching the end with a measure of satisfaction, participation, and clarity that would appear to be lacking if everything were laid out cold at first in the contract. What, then, about the times when you most explicitly do *not* want the outcome of a sermon known in advance? That concern is a good reminder that we need to separate the process of participating in a sermon—what we expect of people as a *way of listening*—and the content of the message itself. A contract has to do with the former, with the process itself, rather than with the content. Asking people to join a thinking-through process, trying to work toward a point that we will not know about until we get there, or seeking to find a hidden meaning are all contract-setting messages that leave the discovery dynamic intact so far as content is concerned. They are most assuredly *not* the same as that old bromide about content, "Tell 'em what you're going to tell 'em, then tell 'em, then tell 'em what you told 'em." If we want to take people on a kind of journey through a problematic subject, all to the good; but let us tell them that is what we want and ask for the help of their imaginations and their personal experiences as we go. (On the whole, though, preachers would probably do well to be at least a little suspicious of "surprise endings." What they seem to gain in drama, they have a way of losing in digestibility.)

The second objection to such an emphasis on contract setting arises from a concern, entirely appropriate in and of itself, to create a well-spoken or well-written message that is, frankly, a thing of beauty. Does not a lot of rather awkward metacommunicative talk—"Here is what we are trying to do, and as we go along will you think of your own experience? And, yes, it is tough but we need to tackle it, and it is not going to be comfortable saying or hearing this, but"—does not all that pretty badly maim what would otherwise be a literate piece of communication? Yes and no. Let us assume that the raiser of that objection has not gotten confused about the purpose of preaching compared to the writing of immortal essays, and that the point is cogent. There truly *are* times when to stop and speak a metacommunicative aside would be disruptive. Probably those times are not as frequent as most of us might tend to fear, but they do happen.

Take, for instance, the so-called first-person sermon, in which the preacher takes the role of some biblical character and speaks in the first person as though he or she were that character talking. When properly done, a first-person sermon is a graceful creation that should not be tampered with. In such cases, of which the first-person sermon is but one example, we need to think in terms of an "interpretative frame" around the sermon, a period of straight metacommunicative talk before and/or after the main body of content, in which our contract setting and interpretation is done. For some reason, preachers are forever forgetting that the sermon is not the only place in a worship service where they speak directly to people. Some of the most effective contract setting for preaching has been done at other points in the worship service besides the time of the sermon itself, starting with the Call to Worship and earlier.

Even the lowly church bulletin can have a part to play in the process. It does not have to be limited to announcing parish events forthcoming and the bare-bones order of worship. There is no reason a printed bulletin cannot speak directly to people about the worship experience they have now come for, in either paragraph notes or rubrics within the order of worship.

To come back to the example, there is no good reason to believe that introducing, let us say, a first-person sermon in plain English, telling people what you are doing and why, and asking them to join in the process, somehow ruins it. Quite the contrary: starting such a sermon without appropriate contract setting will cost a few minutes of confusion and anxiety in hearers, with corresponding dilution of whatever the preacher was trying for.

Aside from the opportunities to teach people how to listen within any one sermon and with special ones devoted to that end, there is one other fairly common tool that can be resharpened for the purpose: the "sermon feedback group" of laypeople, either with or without the preacher. Experience varies widely with such groups, but most face a common problem at the outset: people by and large do not want to "criticize" their pastor, no matter how much open encouragement they are given to do so. Yet for some reason most such groups seem to be structured with a view to *helping the preacher* through various forms of critique, feedback, and reaction. Seldom are they used for what they *could* do very well and with willing participation from laypeople; namely, teach people how to participate in the preaching experience, how to listen to a sermon.

Particularly if a just-completed sermon has aimed pastorally at helping people in some aspects of their living and thinking, it is a wrenching change of agenda to ask those same people now to assume the stance of critics, rather like that sick old one-liner, "Other than that, Mrs. Lincoln, how did you like the play?" Feedback is an important part of the communication process, to be sure; but the way it is used with so-called sermon feedback groups is often naive if not crass. The most telling feedback after, let us say, a moving pastoral sermon, might well be a layperson's refusal to pick a personally important event apart intellectually.

It is really quite easy to take the sting of criticizing the preacher or of violating a personal experience out of a sermon discussion group. All it requires is for the preacher to establish a contract with the group that makes clear that the agenda is intended to discuss and enrich their experience of the sermon, whatever it might be, *without* evaluative judgments on its quality (and willy-nilly, on its author). If the preacher-leader's organizing idea for the group is "How can we all learn better how to hear, understand, and respond to the preaching experience?" rather than, "How good or bad was my sermon?" a very different group communication experience will result. It can be yet another tool for teaching people how to listen to preaching. Naturally the preacher will get useful information that will feed into the sermon preparation process; but the focus of the group will not be on judgment or on the preacher, but on the "preaching event" in all its strangeness and complexity.

Chapter 17. **Company Coming**

Try as we will to get away from privatizing or individualizing the intentions of preaching, we continually have a difficult time with the corporate, communal, koinonia aspects of our work in the pulpit. We worry a great deal about "building community," and we fervently hope that somehow preaching will call out the people into a sense of koinonia. But what the connections might be between "preaching and congregation," to use Von Allmen's title, often remain obscure.[1] "How can we preach so as to build community in our people?" is both a perennial favorite and a stubbornly persistent mystery in homiletical discussions. It will not be solved here, but it may help to get us farther down the line to say that *putting the question that way has been to ask the wrong question.*

The truth is, preaching cannot help but create communities of *some* kind; the real question is *what* kind will they be? This is a somewhat complicated idea that can be illustrated by another domain of communication activity, for application to preaching.

Students of mass media think in terms of "publics," which are the receiving end of mass media communication of all kinds. William Stephenson has argued that one of the primary functions of the newspaper is not so much conveying information as it is creating and sustaining various kinds of such "publics."[2] A public is a group of people, scattered or localized, who are bound together in some respect by a common interest, set of values, or cause. We are all members of different publics simultaneously. We may be the news-reading public, or the automobile-buying public or the public crusading against nuclear reactors. At a PTA meeting, I am part of the public of parents-of-children-in-this-school; at a faculty meeting, I am a member of the teaching-ministers-in-training public, and so it goes. *One of the primary functions of communication is to create publics,* and you could even say with a little stretching that even the most intimate, one-to-one communication has as one of its dominant dynamics the creation of a public consisting of you-and-me-together in some shared purpose, no matter how fleeting. Publics are sometimes short-lived, sometimes long-running; sometimes large and sometimes very small; sometimes known to each other and other times widely scattered.

That part of communication behavior that serves to create publics is often hidden from the most obvious part of the message. It is found in such things as the selection of this topic rather than that one, phrasing a point one way but not another, emphasizing certain things and playing others down, choosing a synonym of a different connotation from its semantic neighbor, and so forth through the subtle intricacies of language and form. It is a systemic, sometimes unconscious, pervasive cluster of beliefs and values that are carried along with the message like the unnoticed riders to a bill in Congress.

Again the domain of mass media provides a good illustration. Take automobile advertisements, for instance. Particularly in the fall, when new models come out, the ads in a national magazine will be fiercely competitive in their attempts to persuade you that a Belchfire is superior to a Lurchmobile. On the local scene, dealers outdo themselves in newspaper and television ads to convince us that the good life, if not life itself, will be drastically foreshortened unless we trade with them. Obviously those messages carry information about Belchfires, Lurchmobiles, prices, good deals, safety features, and all the other impedimenta of auto ads. What is not so obvious is that entirely apart from the concrete persuasive information of the ads is yet another dimension of the message. It is a systemic and hidden one, which fundamentally says something like, "Unless you become a member of the car-buying public, *never mind which kind or from whom,* you will be missing something of value." From a systematic point of view, in other words, the most significant impact of the message is not on whether you buy one kind of car from one dealer or another, but rather on the importance of your buying a new car, *period.* George Gerbner has explained it in terms of the function of communication in *cultivating* certain beliefs and values, prior to communication's role in persuading certain *changes* in the particulars of those underlying assumptions.[3] You have to get below the surfaces of messages to see that. Social psychologists have discovered, for instance, that the most attentive reading of automobile ads is found in people who have *just purchased* an automobile. The function of the ad, contrary to common assumption, is not entirely to persuade them to make a choice, but equally (if not more) to ease the inevitable anxiety of already having made a choice and wanting to be assured it was the right one—to make them more solidly comfortable as members of the just-bought-a-car public.[4]

To see how the public-forming idea works in communication, take a look at messages designed for different reading publics but with essentially the same information or message, say the description of a new prescription drug. A drug's publicity brochure given to physicians or an ad placed in a medical journal describes the product with a view to persuading the physician to use it on patients in his or her care. The write-up on the same drug that appears in the *Physicians' Desk Reference,* an encyclopedic reference book about medications, is much different. A report on the product in one of the health magazines written for laypeople is different still. If by chance the drug has a controversial aspect and is written about by critics the same information will take yet a different turn. One way of thinking about the differences among those messages is to realize that each different message is based on the assumption of a certain kind of actual or potential receiving public: physicians who may prescribe the drug in the first case; physicians or medical students who have already decided to consider using the drug in the second; laypeople who may be given the drug (or who may press their doctors for it) in the third instance, and potential critics or protesters of the drug in the last message.

Advertising is not so very far from preaching, strange as it may seem. Sermons too are built on some assumptions about the kind of "publics" who will be hearing them, although those assumptions may be hidden even from the preacher writing the sermon. The communication principle here is that a receiver automatically "places" himself or herself into some kind of public simply in order to make sense of the incoming message. It may be very clear to me as I listen to a sermon that it is treating me as though I were a member of the public of pleasure seekers who give no thought for the morrow, or as though I were an emotional casualty who needed help, or as though I were one on whose money the church could depend for its survival. There is a sense, then, in which I have to envision myself at least as a pretending member of such a public simply in order to make sense of what is being said. I have to answer for myself the question, "Who am I to be hearing this message and understanding it in this way?" It happens without thought or effort; it is the way communication works.

We would do well not to worry so much about whether our preaching "builds communities," because in the sense of creating publics it cannot help but do it. Our concern really ought to be more for what *kind* of community we are cultivating by aiming our sermons toward it.

The dynamic of public formation in preaching can be observed especially clearly when circumstances bring a large number and variety of preachers to preach on the same thing at about the same time—whether it be Easter Day or an event in the news. An arresting and important occasion of that nature was the controversy among United Presbyterians in the early summer of 1971 over their denomination's granting of $10,000 from its legal defense fund for poor and minority people to Angela Davis, an avowed Communist accused of murder. A group of Presbyterians had successfully appealed to the fund on her behalf and the grant was revealed at the United Presbyterian General Assembly, the denomination's annual national judicatory meeting. It made quick and sensational public news and rocked Presbyterian congregations across the country to their foundations. Within a two-week period probably most Presbyterian preachers treated the "Angela Davis controversy" in their sermons in some fashion or other.

Little research has been done on the communicative dimension of that complex skein of events and reactions, but it serves as almost a paradigm of the public-forming dimension of preaching, as of any communication. A Princeton graduate student undertook to examine a sampling of preaching related to that event.[5] The results were interesting in several ways, including, of course, what they showed about the variety of different positions, partisan and nonpartisan, that preachers took on the matter. Congregations and preachers were frequently at odds with each other, and it is safe to say that everybody was on the outs with somebody else in the denomination.

As sermon samples began to accumulate in the research, however, what began to prove most interesting was not the obvious controversy but the public-forming aspect of the preaching involved; not, in other words, what various preachers said or whether they were for or against the grant, but rather what kinds of communities were being both assumed and built, subliminally if you will, by preaching that for the most part *thought* its main agenda was the conscious issue of the grant itself. Sermons could be divided into at least five separate categories based not on the positions taken (which could be diametrically opposed *within the same category,* from this perspective) but on the kinds of publics that could be assumed to underlie the preachers' intentions. There were (1) sermons that assumed a congregation of protesting partisans, whether the preacher aimed to calm or incite them; (2) sermons that addressed people as though they were primarily seeking to gather information and understand precisely what had happened to whom and under what circumstances; (3) sermons that were beamed at people who were dominantly concerned with their denominational affiliation and what that both meant and mandated, negatively or positively, (4) sermons whose receiving public was assumed to be theologically defined around the issue of what it means for us to "do justice" in the biblical-theological sense, and (5) sermons that spoke to people as though they were wounded and in need of healing. Few of these "Angela Davis sermons" thought consciously about what kind of public they were assuming and/or trying to cultivate. Most people looked at the most visible issues and organizational dynamics.

In a related dimension of those events, boxes and boxes of statements from congregations, church sessions, and ministers were received by the United Presbyterian General Assembly headquarters office, most of them making some point or other and all of them, willy-nilly, expressing their constituents' "public" position. Here we have the protruding tip of a minor para-

ble: those crates of documents were most likely never read by
their intended receivers at denominational headquarters. At
last report, several years later, they remained unsorted and
unnoticed in a jumble of cartons in a denominational storage
area. Does that mean they were wasted communicative effort?
By no means. They, like the sermons, were part of the public-
forming process of their originators, a way for groups of concerned people to articulate just who they thought they were—
the very same dynamic that is found in the Angela Davis preaching. There is a sense, in other words, in which the intended
receivers of those documents were the groups themselves that
authored them, not the denominational officials at all.

If we asked, then, "How can preaching on this issue build
community?" we would be asking an unnecessary, dead-end
question. If we shifted the perspective and asked, "What kind
of community was nurtured in and through the process of this
preaching?" we would observe part of the inner communicative
dynamics of preaching at its most powerful—and most hidden.

In the sermon-planning process we will talk about in more
detail in the next section, one of the key questions the preacher
is asked to answer in preparing a sermon is what kind of people
would be the ideal listeners to this particular sermon. What sort
of public a preacher wants to create allows us to go the next step
and ask whether the sermon does what its author wants it to or
not. It may be that while a preacher wanted to treat the congregation as the public of "people who have just received an unexpected gift," the sermon *in fact* worked toward cultivation of the
public of "convicted felons up for parole." One of the most
common discoveries preaching students make in their seminary homiletics courses is that the public they wanted to nurture
is a far cry from what the sermon (and they themselves, unwittingly) in fact assumed.

We have long valued the practice of imagining a certain hearer or reader as a guide to producing something like a sermon
(or a book about preaching, for that matter). The principle of
public formation takes that idea seriously as an integral part of

the planning of a sermon, rather than a matter of writing style or felicity of expression. The public envisioned for this book, for instance, is made up largely of preachers (and preaching students) who want to evaluate and improve their preaching in somewhat different ways than they would using standard homiletical textbooks. It will also have a much smaller public of critics who are trying to find out whether to recommend this book or not. By sheer fact of reading this, you are a member of the public of readers of this book, with its smaller subpublics of readers who find it exciting, obnoxious, dull, or what have you. Another way of looking at it is to say that you as a reader have already been made a member of a public whether you like it or not; namely, the public of people who have thought about preaching in this fashion. No, I did not fool you or manipulate you or con you, at least not consciously. It is just the way the communication process works—to create publics of many different kinds. Most of you will in turn be building a community when you preach next Sunday. You do not have to worry whether or not you are; you should reflect on what kind of community you cultivate no matter whether your sermon is inspired or dull, eloquent or fumbling, relevant or prehistoric.

There is some risk in this talk about publics that we will become technical or mechanical in speaking about what is at bottom a theological reality—the formation of community. That would be a serious mistake, and this is a warning against making it. Writing about community for some reason usually runs the risk of trivialization, probably just because the potential for its importance is so high and we have a way of not knowing quite what to do with such things. For now, let it be said that public formation in the communicative sense or the building of community in theological perspective is always both more and less than it seems—more important, more long-lasting, more influential; and less conscious, less understandable, and less immediate. Once you were no people, scripture says, and now you are God's (I Pet. 2:10). *That* is what is going on, call it what we will. For the preacher to be involved in that genesis as herald, midwife, critic, or whatever means at the very least that the preaching task is never even in its most technical and trivial moments separated from its theological foundation.

That much, at least, should be in preachers' minds as they think about their work: that in ways they will for the most part never directly see or know about their work is a part of the life-determining process wherein people come together into community, lots of communities, really. Communities have homes to live in, and the image of building a sermon turns out to be not so far from the plain truth after all.

V

BACK TO THE DRAWING BOARD
Methods That Work

Every theater has its "green room" where actors and friends meet in the rare euphoria of a performance just completed. That is where we are now. The sermon has been built. We have talked about purposes, about preparation, about tools and materials, about the people who receive our work. We have, I hope, learned some things; and since the preacher's task is a cycle, week in and week out, we are inevitably back to the drawing board. The purpose of this section is to speak very pragmatically about the task now before us, preparing next week's sermon, which we have looked at theologically and communicatively in preceding pages. None of what we have said and thought through will matter much if it does not enter the mix of the preacher's preparation and work, however, and in the following five chapters we want to help that appropriative process with some concrete methods. They all work; but they will not all suit everyone, certainly not in the exact form in which they appear here. You should know, though, that each of them has been given a healthy field testing in the practice of preachers much like yourselves. Not to put too fine a point to it, they all came initially out of my own practice, were sharpened in dialogue with hundreds of other ministers in classes, seminars, and continuing education groups, and have been updated as people have let me know in return how they worked.

Chapter 18. Power Planning

Everyone has a sermon-planning method.[1] It may be utterly chaotic, intuitive, or unconscious, but everyone has one. There really is no escaping it. Readers ought to know that before reading about the sermon-building procedure I am going to talk about, because whatever their method is now will certainly color their reaction to the suggestion of a new one. That is fine; most bright ideas about sermon planning come to grief, I am convinced, because they advertise themselves as giving something the readers did not have before (and assume they ought to be grateful), when that is plainly not the case. This method, then, while it can be used as is if readers choose to set whatever else they do aside, will more likely go into the mix of what they now do, hope to do, cannot do, and ought to do. I hope it will thereby do ministers and their hearers some good. Readers should take it apart and use it however and to what extent they wish.

My reason for including it is twofold. First, it gathers up several theoretical ideas talked about in earlier pages that we tend to neglect in our preaching preparation—things such as the narrative theme of a sermon, its contract with listeners, and its public-forming dynamic. The method is not primarily rhetorical or stylistic, and it will not really help you much with the concrete business of writing a sermon. It does, however, try to keep a preacher in touch with some of the underlying communication dynamics of the sermon, which is where most methods seem to fall short.

Second, the "power planning" method uses the same set of criteria for building a sermon as for evaluating one later, and strangely enough that is something seldom done. Without paying much attention to it, homileticians have gotten into the bad habit of using one set of criteria to guide the construction of a sermon, and then another set for evaluating the outcome. When we sit down to write a sermon, we ask such questions as, "Have I condensed the central thrust of the biblical text to one main proposition?" but then at the other end we look back on the finished product and wonder, "Was the language vivid and engaging? Were the points clear? Did it hold the congregation's interest?"

There would seem to be some value in hooking those two sets of questions together so that what we aim to do in preaching can be looked at after the fact (either of preparation or of preaching) to see whether we made it or not. This method, then, is just as much a sermon evaluation guide as it is a planning process.

The underlying image of "power planning" is gnostic, not energetic: it comes from a microscope's lens turret with its three lenses for increasing degrees of magnification—ten, twenty, and thirty power usually. The basic notion is that you can look at the sermon-building process through three degrees of lens power. Ten power is the broadest overview, giving you a look at the whole specimen. Twenty power takes you in a notch closer, with emphasis on the movement from text to sermon strategy. Thirty power is the most penetrating; it scans for communication dynamics in theological perspective.

Some preachers like the idea of a worksheet for each sermon. It has the advantage of portability as well as neatness, to say nothing of keeping a record of weekly preaching for file and index purposes. A worksheet somehow pronounces a benediction of order on the motley assortment of scribblings, newspaper clippings, backs of old envelopes, and paper napkins that make up some of our usual sermon files. The bottom part of the worksheet on the following page (which readers are free to duplicate for their own use) harvests the fruits of the power-planning process. The top of the sheet is for more general weekly information, some of which we tend to neglect.

Some of the worksheet items may not be self-explanatory. The item *Liturgical calendar* means, of course, which Sunday of the church year this particular sermon is going to be preached on—first in Lent, fourth after Pentecost, Christmas Eve, and so on. Fill in that blank *even if you do not think you have any immediate use for it.* As you look back over your months and years of preaching, you will be surprised how handy it becomes to be able to locate what you preached not on a certain date or topic, but for certain times in the liturgical year. It is obviously useful when planning a series of sermons, say for Lent, to know whether you are looking at the first or the *N*th Sunday. And, not to make too big a thing of it, recording the liturgical calendar is one of those pieces of free information that would take more effort than any of us will spend to go back and retrieve *later*, but which can be had for the asking now.

The item *Special events* refers to events occurring in worship—baptisms, communion, church school teacher recognition, officer installation, or what have you. Someday when you are moved for heaven knows what reason to wonder what you ever preached on all the Sundays when new members were received into the congregation, for instance, you will have the information at hand. The heading *Major recent events*, by contrast, is the place to note down what has been going on in the community, the world, or the congregation that ought to be considered, to one degree or another, in the planning of the sermon. Again, it is a piece of history, not necessarily earth-shaking or even memorable. But that is precisely why it is good to make note of

SERMON PLAN WORKSHEET

Sermon no.: __ Date to be used: __ Liturgical calendar: __

Old Testament: _____ New Testament: _____

Title of Sermon: _____

Hymns: _____ Special events or music: _____

Major recent events: _____

Recurring theme in ministry: _____

Own "life story" connection: _____

Ten-Power Planning (The Preacher)

A. Purpose of sermon (*What do I want to accomplish?*):

B. Theme of sermon (*What will it be a story about?*):

Twenty-Power Planning
(The Preacher and the Passage)

A. Context of passage:	D. Obstacles to communication:
B. Theological subject:	E. Central idea of passage:
C. Point of contact:	F. Sermon idea:

Thirty-Power Planning
(The Preacher, the Passage, and the People)

A. Contract (*What are we doing here?*):

B. Relevance (*Why do I need this?*):

C. Responsibility (*What am I supposed to do?*):

D. Role (*What kind of company am I in?*):

it. It is what influences us subtly at the time but is easily forgotten that we want to keep track of.

The line asking for the preacher's recurring themes in ministry can be linked with the basic inventory of ideas discussed earlier in Chapter 10 and taken up again in Chapter 19, following this one. Each preacher can phrase it any way that seems accurate and workable. It can be used also as a more task-oriented item reflecting working goals a preacher has for his or her ministry in a particular setting. Whichever, that item is important because *some* major theme of importance to us is going to be operative in the conception, planning, and bringing off of a sermon in its worship context, and not knowing what frequency we are navigating by is flying blind. The fabled and fuddled one-idea preacher who becomes groaningly predictable week after week may not be suffering so much from a lack of ideas as from a *lack of awareness* of what ideas are being used. The preaching is concentrated in a more narrow band of thinking than even he or she would like. Since my own work, for instance, tends to place heavy emphasis on the pastoral and psychotherapeutic aspects of ministry, I have to use that line of the worksheet as a way of coming clean on what I am *not* saying, and then of disciplining myself to cover all the bases of my concerns—a kind of theological menu planning.

The last general bit of information on the worksheet uses the by now cliché language of "my own story." Probably that could be changed to something like, "What of pivotal importance to me as a person is being expressed?" without losing anything in the translation. Still, the "story" idea has a solid core even if it may shortly need to be pruned of overexuberant top growth. We do well to give up a pretense to detached objectivity in preaching. It would not be any good even if it were possible, which it is not. Far better for us to be realistically and self-critically in touch with the plots and characters and values that make up the lived-out biography of the person of the preacher, than to try to pretend we have got beyond all that. Knowing, for instance, that a main theme of my own "story" is a lifelong search for zones of quiet and of simple, reliable beauty in an age that fates me to deal with more noise, complexity, uncertainty, and practicality than I would like, is a realistic way of keeping in touch with something that both shapes my perception of things and lets me get close to other people in certain ways. Knowing that keeps me focused and hopeful and at the same time realistic in detecting the scatteredness and pessimism that never gives up trying to steal the scene.

Few people will fill out this worksheet item neatly following item, like a credit application. Part of the beauty of having your own sermon method already is just that you can and should roam back and forth through this power-planning process in whatever way is native to you, letting one category inform another as you go. In preaching, as in working jigsaw puzzles, it is hard to learn there is no one right way to do it. Dad insists on getting all the border pieces together first; Mom works on the principle of putting one figure in the scene together at a time; No. 1 daughter gathers her pieces together by shade of color, and Junior (who is fated to become either a psychiatrist or a plumber) goes inexorably for matching shapes of the cut-outs themselves. Sooner or later, they all get the puzzle done. The only advice that might be given is that in general it makes sense to work in "sweeps" from lesser to greater power, so that in the end one can read a completed power-planning worksheet as the logical, unfolding development of a sermon, no matter how illogically it *got* that way.

TEN-POWER PLANNING

Purpose

Sermon planning can begin with being able to say, in a single sentence, what you want the sermon to accomplish in terms of your people's behavior, feelings, or experience. Please read that sentence again, because experience has shown it to be

virtually certain its meaning will *not* be clear at once. The statement of the purpose of the sermon is not the ideational content
of the sermon, its "topic sentence," or "basic proposition," or
"core idea." No, *purpose* describes *what you want to have happen*
with this sermon. Borrowing the language of education, purpose should describe a "behavioral objective" of the sermon,
an outcome that one can somehow get a look at (at least in
theory) and answer the question, "Well, did it happen or not,
and how could I tell the difference?" Try as they will, not one
seminary student in ten is able on the first try to write out a
statement of purpose that is observable enough, limited
enough, and down to earth enough to suffice. Practicing
preachers are not much better. We get sentences such as "For
people to understand that God's grace is freely given," which
immediately and automatically fates the preacher to being unable to tell whether the sermon accomplished its purpose or
not—"understanding" being a phenomenon as little observable as "grace" and as hard to recognize when it happens. Why
not instead, "For people to identify experiences in their lives
when they got more than they deserved, and to see them as
examples of the way God works." This one came along the
other day: "The purpose of this sermon is for people to know
the joy of the Lord throughout their beings and in all creation."
A hymn, maybe; a sermon purpose, no. It *might* be "This sermon aims to help people feel joyful, especially about some
things they had been matter-of-fact about before." A particular
favorite started out this way: "This sermon cultivates in people
an appreciation of tͱe Christian perspective on existence and
what it means." Afteͬ a good deal of arm wrestling, it became
"As a result of this sermon, I want people not to use the word
Christian as an adjective for one week without stopping to think
what it might mean."

Do not think that in recasting a sermon's aspirations into the
mundane language of communicative accomplishment we have
drained all the theology out. The greater enemy for theological
awareness is *more* abstruse theological conceptualization, not

less. It is one thing, as I noted in Chapter 12, to use theological language to interpret the connectedness and significance of things, to "refer them to God";[2] it is something else again to try to make the interpretative language of theological conceptualization serve as descriptive, empirical talk about the living, acting, feeling, judging, wishing, relating experiences that make up our days. In a statement of purpose, we are after the description, leaving the theological interpretation to follow as it must and should, but not confusing the two.

Another troubling wrinkle to the idea of a sermon's purpose is quite simply that something as flat and mundane as a purpose just does not seem to match the importance or depth of the investment we have in a sermon. It feels like a loss, a dilution, a settling for something ordinary when what we had in mind was really quite moving and special. It is almost as though we feared leaving the fire of creativity untended for even a moment lest it go out, forgetting that in order to get to be a fire at all it has to come in contact with the ordinary, quite possibly green, kindling of its fuel. Perhaps there was a time, and will be again, when preaching was so deadly mundane and specific that it needed all the spiritual awakening that art and devotion could give it. What is needed now, though, is a new appreciation of how sermons gain, not lose, their power, subtlety, and effectiveness by starting with direct, plain thought about what a preacher wants to see happen and why.

Theme

Now the planning process can think about sermon content rather than experiential outcome. But there is another difference from the usual practice, to be negotiated at the ten-power level. Try to think of the sermon as a story, without getting too fancy about it, and then answer the question: What is this sermon a story *about*? The operative word is *about*. It serves to orient us in the narrative, rather than the speculative, direction that preaching needs to go. A sermon whose text is the feeding of 5,000 people might be "a story about how people could not see something they really wanted even when it was staring them in the face." A sermon focusing on Peter's courtyard denial of Jesus might be "a story about one man's discovery that under pressure he sold out the one person he swore he could be true to, to the end." A sermon built on the "Who can separate us from the love of God?" passage of Romans 8, no matter how poetic and theological it will be as a message, could nevertheless be "a story about how from somewhere God survives for us as God when we have given up all realistic hope."

Again the emphasis of the story theme is on the people's experience and what the preacher hopes it will be. Talking about the theme of a sermon in story form does not mean that the sermon itself will take any particular rhetorical or stylistic form. Even the most philosophical of sermons is a story about something in the foundational sense that any message reports at the very least its author's experience of value, connectedness, reality, and rightness about the subject matter.[3]

To sum up: Ten-power planning does not give you a sermon, still less an outline. It gives you an explicit purpose for this particular message, and an articulated sense of what the theme of this message will be as it enters the domain of our experience. Some preachers will have chosen a text as the basis on which to begin ten-power planning; others or the same ones at other times will at this point have neither text nor any clue as to the sermon's development. Use whatever method works for you, subject of course to the hard-nosed hermeneutical questions about you, a text, and your sermon that never get set aside no matter what procedure we adopt. Ten-power planning can, if you wish, stop there temporarily, giving the foundation for a sermon to be developed later. You can plan a series or a year's worth of sermons if you wish, taking them all to the ten-power stage for overall planning purposes, and continuing the process through later phases when the time is right for each.

TWENTY-POWER PLANNING

Twenty-power planning is primarily concerned with the preacher's work on a biblical text as the basis for a sermon. Obviously it is less relevant to types of preaching where a text is less central, all the way to what used to be called "topical preaching" (even though biblical texts were usually somewhere involved even in those kinds of sermons, as witness Fosdick, whose so-called topical sermons were as biblically based as you could wish). How the text has been chosen is not essential to twenty-power planning; even if the preacher has selected the text eisegetically, the twenty-power process involves us in a hermeneutical dialogue with the text in which our own concerns and preunderstandings are both taken seriously, and also recast under the influence of the text's witness.

The six stages of twenty-power planning *are* meant to be taken in order, even if the twenty-power segment as a whole is not. The final stage, "Sermon Idea," is the payoff, so to speak, the likelihood being that having gone through the preceding five steps a preacher will by the end have come to some at least potential crystallizations of meaning and impact that can be called "sermon ideas." The notion of using stages like this is an adaptation of an informal procedure used by the late Paul Scherer in his preaching classes. Scherer used to require that students fold a letter-size sheet of paper lengthwise, draw a line down the middle, complete a five-stage exegetical format on one half, and then make beginning sermon notes on the other. Length was strictly limited to whatever one could cram into that 8½ × 11-inch area, and not even the compulsive ingenuity of wordy seminarians who used margins never before discovered could cancel out the underlying value of the procedure: when you had the heart of an exegetical process condensed into that compass, you were living in the text in the only way that ever did lead to good preaching. Nothing I have ever seen has improved the device. I have updated the way the categories are phrased; the underlying genius remains the same, and it is Scherer's.

Context of the Passage

What is the text's context *historically* in the biblical chain of events? The calls of Isaiah, Moses, Amos, the disciples, Paul, and John are similar, for example, but their historical contexts are obviously different. What are they? Next, what is the text's context *scripturally* or *editorially;* that is, where does it fall in the biblical writing and why? Does the meaning of a parable shift because Luke embeds it in one context and Matthew in another? Suppose, for instance, that in one biblical setting Jesus' saying is in context of rejection by an unsympathetic crowd hearing him, while in another book the same saying has for its context an adulation that wanted to make Jesus king. Which was acceptance and which rejection, theologically speaking? Hard to say, perhaps, but the main thing is that the question would never even arise (nor the sermon that obviously could take off from this point alone) except by noticing the text's scriptural or editorial context.

Theological Subject

Here, at last, is where the preacher is licensed to use those theological code words that the prior pages have sometimes been hard on. Applying our usual theological categories, under which one would this text probably be indexed if, say, one were reading a "theological-topical index of biblical texts"? Bear in mind that we are using highly condensed and potent chemical solutions here. It is not that the passage itself intended to have this or that theological heading; the question is how might *we* classify it? Vocation? Salvation? Knowledge of God? Nature of the church? God's will? Theology of history? Christ and culture? Grace? The problem of evil? And so on through the long litany of theological conceptual categories that serve an indexing and interpretative but not a descriptive function.

The purpose of this kind of classifying is not to shoehorn a text into a theological mold or to lay an interpretative template over it. It is, rather, to begin to connect the narrative or poetic or historical content of a text with the ways of thinking the Christian tradition has used to make sense of itself. The chances are very good that the theological code used in this place in the planning will never appear explicitly in the sermon itself; that is not the purpose. The point is that we cannot help but look at a text from some theological perspective or other, and it pays to become self-conscious about which one is operative at the time. The same text will probably fall under several categories potentially. It is not that one is "right," but rather that one is dominant in this interpretation, another in that. One of the most important points in the methodology of biblical interpretation, arguable to be sure, is that texts are multidimensional and multivalent in their meaning. There is no single, cast-in-bronze interpretation or even meaning that excludes all others. Nor, of course, are biblical texts exercises in interpretative projection, a sort of Judaeo-Christian Rorschach test. The truth falls in between, in the variety of dimensions or aspects to a text, and the variety of ways a text connects with other things. A text is rather like the gregarious carbon atom, if my dim memory of chemistry serves, which combines with other elements in a variety of ways to make everything from industrial diamonds to club soda.

Point of Contact

The phrase "point of contact" is Bultmann's, originally. Where does the text touch our personal concerns?[4] What sort of personal question can you assume in order to hear the passage as address or answer? Is there some innovation, human condition, conflict, life-determining value, feeling, or issue going on with us that brings us into the lived world that lies behind this passage? It pays to think of a biblical text as the attempt at some point in time by some living people to record or thematize[5] an aspect of their profoundest religious experience. Sometimes the motivating context of that experience is plain to us;

more often, not. Thinking of the text as someone's attempt to reflect on the answer to some important question brings us into the world of the text at the same level: What might the point of contact be for us too?

A twofold danger arises when talking about point of contact, and indeed the phrase itself is disputed by neoorthodox theologians who deny the existence of any such thing, humankind and God being who they each are.[6] We do have to be careful, on the one hand, not to use the Bible as a cookbook of recipes for the sundry appetites and deficiencies that present themselves daily to the preacher. The text is not going to talk about the gasoline crisis or rebellious teenagers or what to do with beloved, senile Aunt Nel. There is a limit to the depths of even a sacred text. But, on the other hand, it would be just as serious a hermeneutical mistake to assume that the surface details of a text are the limit of its agenda, making it largely irrelevant to us. Probably a great deal of the history of biblical interpretation could be seen as attempts to steer between the shoals of those two distortions, the one an overgeneralizing, the other too severe a limitation. Point of contact is somewhere in between, somewhere below the surface of a text, but not too far below the impact of our own existential concerns.

To take a little-used text as illustration, consider Mordecai and Esther's note passing in Esther 4 and 5. Esther says essentially that if she approaches the king she may be killed for speaking out of turn, while her uncle Mordecai reminds her that she is still a Jew no matter how far up the Persian social ladder she has moved as the king's wife. "And who knows," he adds, "whether you might have come to the kingdom for just such a time as this" (Esther 4:14b).

On the surface, it looks like an anguished, but provincial, issue largely unrelated to anything we might face these days. To try to find a point of contact on the surface of the text would be ludicrous—rather like saying that the text teaches us we ought to get out and vote for the reform candidate even at the risk of pneumonia on a bitter November day. But when you direct your gaze to the text slightly beneath the surface you find it talking about such things as a God who is known to reveal himself in the unlikeliest of situations; or a shift of perspective that begins to worry about different things from those it used to, and grows more concerned with being faithful in the critical time than with saving its skin; or a sense of oneself that is defined not so much by the circumstances in which you find yourself as by the things you are willing to die for—if there are any. At *that* level, there is a point of contact, several in fact, with the modern hearer. The important thing to keep in mind in sermon planning is to be skeptical both of the mundane surface and of the unfathomable depths of either the text's or our experience. Just below the surface, though, lies the stratum of recurring existential questions and concerns that come with the human species, taking the immediate form and shape of this everyday issue and that, but of the house and lineage of articulate human experience everywhere—particularly in the Bible.

Obstacles to Communication

What makes a text difficult to talk about, read, or understand? What are the obstacles we will face as we try to make our way through it? Preachers need here to set aside temporarily some of the arcane knowledge with which they have become equipped through training and experience. Thinking like the person in the pew, they must ask what is it that makes this text tough enough that a newspaper editor would send it back for a rewrite? Perhaps the historical context is too foreign or too complicated. You cannot very well cover in one sermon several hundred years of fighting that lie behind the text—but you cannot make much sense of the Battle of Jericho without them.

Maybe there are nonrational or extraordinary factors in the text that need interpretation, all the way from miracles and natural wonders to the very poetic form of a text itself. They do not have to be explained away; but they do have to be taken into account as obstacles to communication, immediate or potential. More subtle, but just as lethal for communication, are questions a text may ask that appear to be too far removed from our frame of reference. "What must I do to be saved?" the text asks, and hundreds of preachers throughout history have begun their sermons with some such headline as "All of us here today are asking in our own ways what we can do to ensure our salvation." Well, leaving aside the occasional religious fanatic, most of us never heard *anyone* ask anything remotely close to that. It is positively amazing the way preachers without thinking about it put the strangest and most esoteric theological questions into the mouths of their constituents, who often as not are too meek or too baffled to protest.

On the other side of the coin, though, maybe a text is just too close for comfort to our own situation, and that too is an obstacle to communication. You would have to be either a poet or a fool to preach on "The wages of sin are death" on a Sunday morning when a carful of the congregation's teenagers was killed in an accident after last Saturday night's drinking spree. Less dramatically, preachers need to learn to recognize in advance factors in a text that are likely to trigger resistance because they hit too near home.

Finally, there are linguistic obstacles that occasionally have to be met head on—obscure phrases and terms, aphorisms whose popular meaning in the time of the text needs to be understood, and so on. Occasionally there will even be translation problems, which will drive a preacher back to the commentaries, if not to the original language. (A warning sounded by James Barr deserves repeating, though, that biblical texts rely far less for their meaning on pregnant terms and nuances of the Greek or Hebrew "minds" than preachers are prone to claim. The "word study" approach, whose highest expression is the Kittel Dictionary, can itself become an obstacle to communication;[7] most congregations are well within their rights in tuning out preachers who launch themselves into supernaturally dull expositions of the term *love* or *sin* or what have you, complete with transliterations of Greek and Hebrew and dire warnings not to think for a minute that the text might have meant plainly what it *said*.)

Central Idea of a Passage

At this point in twenty-power planning, the preacher's familiarity with a text should have grown to the point that a single idea can be articulated that ties the passage together. What is its "central proposition," the inner thread of its meaning? Even more important, can the preacher phrase that central idea in ordinary language free from theological jargon? Taking the Emmaus Road encounter of Luke 24 as an example, can you say that its central idea is something like, "The people found hope for the presence of Christ just when they hit the rock bottom of their bitter despair?" or, perhaps, "They didn't realize Christ was with them until after it was all over"? Contrast that to a similar formulation overloaded with theological jargon, "Eschatological hope was found in the judgment of crucifixion," or "The knowledge of their salvation came through participation in the mystery of the eucharist."

There has never been anything wrong with the notion of getting a central idea or proposition from a text. What *has* been wrong is assuming there was *only one* and, further, assuming it had to be dressed up theologically to pass muster. Actually, the discipline of focusing a text's import in a single sentence is both useful and legitimate so long as it does not become reductionistic—funneling all a text's meaning or scope into a concept or formulation that, after all, is not itself to be found anywhere in the text.

Sermon Idea

Based on the previous five questions, it is quite likely that now you have the germ of a sermon idea from the text. What is it? You are not at this point after a full-dress sermon outline, nor even necessarily a well-formed central proposition for the sermon itself. What you are searching for is the inner seed for the crystal that will be built around it through further planning, your own creative brooding, and the unpredictable range of happenings, insights, and ironies that keep all of us humble, most particularly when we think we have done such a bang-up job of taming the preaching experience so it will wear the saddle of our planning.

THIRTY-POWER PLANNING

In this most fine-grained look at the sermon under construction, we move away from concentration on the text itself to the more fully developed sermon that is in process of emerging. Thirty-power planning is not a step-by-step plan for building the sermon; no plan can actually do that. What we can do, however, is ask four critical questions to focus and guide the sermon as it develops.

Contract

The first such question has to do with contract as discussed earlier in Chapter 16. What is the implied understanding between you and your congregation about what the purpose of your sermon is? Do you have an "agreement" to look at things in certain ways, to answer certain questions, to assume certain things, to hold certain values, to tolerate certain feelings, in the two-way process of this communication?

Bear in mind that the matter of contract is not an optional extra we bring to writing sermons, but a fundamental dynamic of the communication process. A contract will be operative in any event; your choice is to make it conscious, explicit, and negotiated between you and your people. Otherwise, it will be present at least unconsciously, implicitly, and individually with the possibility of as many different perceptions as there are hearers. To sharpen yourself up a bit, put yourself in the position of a listener who is willing to give you his or her attention but is also conscious of the stewardship of time, and ask as though you were in that role, "Why am I listening to this?"

Relevance

Is it clear to you and to your people what life concerns of theirs and yours this sermon is touching? To what extent, in other words, does the sermon expose a problem area of living, and to what extent does it view such an area in theological perspective, "at full depth"[8] as the saying goes? If the gospel is an answer, just what was the question? Can your congregation identify why they might need to hear what you are saying? For that matter, can you?

It will not hurt to repeat a warning of an earlier chapter: if relevance has to be forced or made, it is probably a lost cause. What is needed here is a clearing away of the underbrush so that shared similarities between a text's or a sermon's concerns and mine as a hearer are evident. As a preacher you cannot *make* me interested in that; but, then again, you really do not need to. What is crucial is that you and I together have a shared sense of what the connections are. Making them plain, not hard-selling them, is the business of preaching.

Responsibility

Does the sermon free people to cope with problems of their lives, care for their neighbors and responsibilities, respond in depth to God's promise of freedom, creativity and love? Does it, to use the formula with which this book began, invite a hearer to a healing process through which we will better and more aggressively be able to carry out our commission as Christian disciples?

The alternatives to responsibility are insidious and frightening. Does the sermon avoid the trap of making people unduly dependent on someone or something at the expense of their own initiative or worth? (One thinks of the preacher who takes pains to assure people that thinking positively about their lives will put things right. When that fails in the face of life's undeniable negatives, what recourse is there but to come back for a recharge, depending on the preacher again and again to "say it isn't so.") Does a sermon avoid making people defensive or depressed or guilty about life? (A sermon that saddles me with direct and personal responsibility for world hunger, an ill that I clearly have not the slightest chance of changing on my own, merely makes me guilty, not responsible. The worst thing that could happen is that I might believe it.)

Does the sermon both confront and support people or does it foster denial of their deepest feelings, hopes, relationships, and experiences? (Speaking of grief, the preacher assures me that as a Christian we have an alternative in the hope for eternity, and before I know it we are nodding assent to the otherwise unbelievable idea that the pain of loss and the anger of separation are somehow not "real" and must be wished away.)

Role

"What kind of company am I in?" is a way of asking what sort of temporary public a listener to your sermon is a member of, as we talked about before. Does the sermon in effect ask your congregation to take the role of therapy group? Lecture classroom? Training session? Theater party? Undecided voters? Convicted felons up for parole? Problem-solving task force? Children at play? Art appreciation tour? Archeologists decoding a new Semitic script? Protest group? Assume for one blissful moment that everything you said in the sermon was believed, felt, acted on, and received *as you intended;* and then ask yourself, "What kind of group would this have to be to be hearing this message and behaving that way?"

Thirty-power planning questions are the part of the total process that can serve most directly as a critique for sermons after their construction. The questions can, for that matter, be used as the agenda of a sermon feedback group, subject to the dire warning given earlier that such groups succeed largely to the extent that they rule out the implied agenda of criticizing the preacher's sermon. As a way of asking people to reflect on their experience in the preaching, though, the four questions are one way into the subject. There is a lot more to be said about preaching, of course, but if we can achieve a basic congruence between the intention of the preacher and the experience of the listener we will surely have come a long way.

Chapter 19. **The Idea Inventory**

The insights of the magic number 7, plus or minus two, in Chapter 10, as a guide to thinking about our thinking in preaching will not do the working preacher much good until they generate an idea *inventory*. Preparing and using such a thing is the subject of this chapter.

Basically the idea inventory is just what it says: a survey and cataloguing of the basic ideas, categories of thought, or underlying assumptions that guide not only our thinking but equally our preaching. Keep in mind that this inventory is not going to be just a listing of all the topics of our preaching or the propositional ideas of our sermons. This one will be a categorization into a limited number of conceptualizations that form the basic map of your own thinking. Here is one way to create it, in six steps.

First, select a group of sermons in sequence that will form the basis of your inventory. The past year's sermons would be a good starting point, although, if you have the time and energy, two or three years' worth would be better.

Step 2 requires two things: a pad of paper, and your willingness *not* to think very much about what you are about to do. When you are set, begin reading quickly through the sermon notes, outlines, or manuscripts of your pile of sermons, one at a time. A quick scan should be enough to bring each one back to mind. Jot down on the pad of paper a single phrase or word (maybe a sentence, if you can resist the temptation to start thinking too much right now) *that describes the focal concern of the sermon.* The list will end up with as many entries as there are sermons in your sample, and they might look something like this:

• Loss of joy
• Crisis brings opportunity

- Mystery
- Demands of the world
- God's healing is different
- Worry—good and bad
- What kids think about God

and so on through whatever your listing will be.

Step 3 is in many ways the hardest; it allows you to start thinking *a little*. (The reason for this insistence on turning off your mind, by the way, is simply that starting to analyze and rationalize too soon about the contents of this batch of sermons will soon take you down one or another primrose path of premature conclusions. What we are trying to do now is only to *observe and report* on the fruits of your thinking, but not yet to analyze them.) Now you should sit back and read through your list several times, beginning to notice groupings of the words, phrases, or sentences that seem to bear a general family resemblance to each other. You might notice, for instance, that out of the 50 to 150 sermons you have annotated, groups or clusters of topics emerge, something like the following set:

- Commitment and dedication
- Personal involvement
- Ministry is for everyone
- Being "for" other people
- Crisis is opportunity
- Disciples—Jesus' calling them
- The meaning of Christian care

All of those topics have a certain as yet unspecified general relationship, having to do with how people respond to their sense of God's purpose for them or something like that. In any event, *those entries seem clearly to be different facets of one underlying category*. Your list will yield several such groupings. Do not try to be terribly specific or exact yet; the purpose is to observe and report what seem to be the beginnings of natural clusters of ideas.

Step 4 is nearly the last. Now you do need to begin to think, but to think more like a detective than a theologian. Go through your list, with its tentative family groupings, and sort them out more carefully according to themes or ideas or master images or underlying thoughts that seem to make these ideas clump together. Perhaps your initial groupings will be a dozen or more, and you will discover that some of them combine under one more central notion. Or perhaps you will have only three or four initial groupings, which on closer inspection break down into six or seven. At the conclusion of this step, the raw material of your inventory is complete. You will have a long list of the topics of your year or more's preaching, grouped into family clusters of sermons that were governed by the same integrating concept or idea, down below the surface of their various specific subject matters. That is the key to the whole business: getting down just below the surface of the variety of preaching to find the more structural ideas or themes.

Step 5 is the final one for the inventory itself. Now go through and name each of the governing ideas that lies behind each cluster of topics. The odds are overwhelming that you will have between five and nine such ideas—seven, plus or minus two. If you have fewer, double-check to be sure you do not have two actually distinct ideas rolled into one; if you have more, check for overlooked combinations that would make for a lower number. Use whatever style of labeling the categories you wish. My own inventory on completion had seven categories, each of which had two labels, one a noun describing the subject matter that was basic to the category, and the second a sentence of direct, second-person address to translate that underlying abstraction into a message form. It looks like this:

Subject	Basic Message
Emotions	"You have feelings."
Coping process	"You try."
Perception	"You make sense."
Action	"You are good for something."

Context	"You belong somewhere."
Cosmos	"You are not alone."
Outcomes	"You can be more."

In this case, theological language was deliberately taken out of the inventory. Another preacher's list might be phrased theologically. The main point is that those seven categories and seven basic messages were what I had to say as a preacher.

Step 6 is a checkup. Using your newly completed idea inventory, go back now through a group of sermons *not* included in the sample you devised the list from, and see whether the categories apply: this sermon falling under one idea, that one under another, and so forth. You may discover, for instance, that as your preaching experience has grown your inventory has shifted, so that either different categories or (more likely) different emphases among the basic categories are found in different periods of preaching. Or you may discover, to your horror, that while you have seven perfectly good ideas, you have only preached on two of them during the last six months.

A special note needs to be added about the sermon that just will not fit—it seems to belong in several categories. When that one comes along, take a good look at it to see whether in fact it *does* divide its attention among several basic ideas. Perhaps it would have been a stronger sermon if it had settled for one thing at a time.

It bears repeating that the idea inventory does not give the preacher a magic new way to prepare sermons, or a fistful of sermon ideas that were not there before. What it does give is a tool for the understanding of a preacher's own most basic resource: his or her own creative appropriation of the gospel through the thinking and reflecting processes that are inalienably and indestructibly each of our own gifts for ministry. One's basic ideas may evolve over the years, but the number we have to work with never gets very large. A minor parable may illustrate the point.

In my checkered career as a gardener, one of the things I like to do best in all the world, I have made use of seven basic hand tools. No one of them takes the place of another. They, like the thought categories, are the basic units of the endeavor. Gardening, like preaching, is my overall concern. The weed chopper clears away what hides the ground and the landscape. The shovel turns over new ground. The pick gets out buried rocks. With a spading fork soil enrichers and amendments are worked into the garden. The rake is used to smooth rough spots, even things out, and break up clods. A three-pronged cultivator takes out weeds and keeps the soil open by preventing crusting. The pruner cuts growth where necessary so that the whole thing pays off. If I were asked to name the basic "ideas" I have, the basic tasks I perform as a gardener instead of a preacher, those are the ones I would list. I may buy many other tools (as my wife is fond of reminding me) but they will all be variations on those same basic implements: an electric weed-whacker is still a weeder; a special bulb planter is a shovel, functionally speaking; and the latest marvel on my tool wall is something called a "swoe," which cannot quite decide whether to be a cultivator or a weeder. As I look over the untamed jungle of weeds, undergrowth, and trees that wants someday to be a landscape, it is rather comforting to realize that there are only seven things I have to do, and seven tools, each with variants to make life interesting, with which to do them. With that inventory of tools and tasks, I can make any kind of garden my imagination permits, and it will feed and satisfy to the full. I will never be bored or useless, no matter how much my back aches. My preaching is no different. It is just that the harvest is far richer and more important.

Chapter 20. **Getting to Know the Clients: Case Studies and Preaching**

There is certainly nothing new about a preacher's envisioning some particular potential receiver of a sermon as a guide to its preparation. Fosdick is reputed to have constructed most of his sermons with one such "ideal hearer" in mind, usually someone with whom he had been in pastoral conversation earlier.[1] Usually, however, we stop this imaginary audience procedure too soon, and keep it at so high a level of abstraction and generality that it serves much less usefully than it might.

Two things prove very difficult to do in imagining a receiver of our messages. For one thing, it is hard for some reason for preachers to think concretely and in detail about their imagined people. We will say to ourselves, "Mr. Jones is an upper-middle-class businessman," thinking we have said something descriptive, instead of "Mr. Jones is vice-president of a small roller-bearing manufacturing company, and makes $37,500 a year." Or we will say, "Mrs. Peabody came from a troubled family situation," instead of, "Mrs. Peabody's father was alcoholic and her mother a hostile and defeated woman, leaving the management of too much responsibility for younger brothers and sisters to Mrs. Peabody from the time she was twelve years old."

The other hard thing to do is to trust a fictitious "case study" to represent anything real and helpful in the sermon construction process. We feel as though we have our fingers crossed when thinking about it, and of course when it comes time to prepare the sermon itself, truth must prevail. The essential message of this chapter, then, is simply: take time to build a concrete "case history" of an imaginary listener and then let that listener's way of hearing and responding be a reliable guide to the sermon construction process.

Although it looks like a gimmick, the case study approach is rooted in some good basic theory, which says essentially that when the paths of the "sacred story" of what we hold ultimate in existence, and our "mundane stories" of everyday life cross, in the tense atmosphere of a looming future, then you get the potential for religious disclosure, insight, the moment of the God–person encounter.[2] The case study can be thought of as a way of mapping that intersection, at least from the mundane side. It is a way for the preacher to cultivate that sense of narrative realism that leaves us hearers with no doubt that *we* are the ones addressed by this word, in all our too-credible humanity.

How do you use a case study in preaching? It can be done at any stage of sermon preparation, although preferably before the final outline or manuscript draft is written. Let us say, for illustration, that the preacher has chosen a text and has a basic approach in mind for preaching on it. It is time for a case study.

The first thing to do is imagine a person, real or fictitious (although most will prefer the latter). Jot down some basic information about the person: name, age, sex, marital status, occupation. Then begins the heart of the case study approach. *Begin to interrogate yourself about this person in as much detail as you can muster,* letting your imagination and free association produce the answers. What was the person's mother like? How many brothers and sisters, and what do they do now? What deaths has the person experienced? What marital troubles? Who is important to this person and why? What does the person do in the church, if anything? Who are the person's enemies and why? What hurts the most? And so on through what is almost guaranteed to be a completely enjoyable imaginary biography of a fictitious person who is destined to become a "prime hearer" of the sermon.

What happens to make the case study work? First, the case study turns loose the energy of un-thought-about imaginary connections as the preacher answers questions about the case study subject. Especially when the answers come fast and furious—as, for example, with a group of preachers doing the exercise together, brainstorming-style—what is being built is not only a fictitious case study, but also a true-to-life picture of things the preacher has in mind, consciously and unconsciously. In that sense, the case study is a kind of projection of the preacher's own concerns and feelings, many of which would be completely hidden by a more rational, deliberate preparation process.

Second, the case study raises the realistic question, "What will the person I am describing make of the sermon I propose to preach?" Where does the sermon need to go to reach a point of contact with such a person? What connections did I myself have in mind, evidently, in order to imagine a hearer as this kind of person? What kind of language, logic, and expression would I use in talking to this person face to face?

Third, the case study gives human form to the objective of a particular sermon, which can now be phrased in direct personal terms as though addressed to the case study person. If the preacher imagines an interview with that person after the sermon is preached, how will we be able to tell whether the sermon accomplished its purpose or not? If we cannot tell, perhaps we had better rethink the purpose. Even prior to that, the case study approach lets the preacher sharpen his or her preaching objective in order to answer the question, "What do I want to happen in John Doe's life as the result of this sermon?"

Finally, the case study heightens the immediacy of the communication of a sermon, in the same sense that Johnny's mother's "Time to come for dinner" message does not do the work with busily playing Johnny until the third time Mom calls, this time with *immediacy*.[3] The circle is thus complete from basic conceptualization through immediate expressive style. The preparation has been guided all along by the critical awareness of direct, conversational address to a flesh and blood human being, no matter how fictitious he or she happens to be.

In time you will devise your own case study format, with questions that yield information particularly useful to you. For now, here is a starter list of blanks to be filled out for a biographical sketch of the preacher's friend, real or imagined:

- Name
- Marital status—include history of divorce or death of spouse
- Children and their ages, health, occupations if applicable
- Occupation—before retirement and after
- Health—include any problems in the past
- Economic situation: compare present to growing-up period; note major changes
- Personality sketch
- Main weaknesses of this person
- Activity in the church
- Major interests besides main occupation
- What do you like most and least about the person?
- The person's theological stance and background in church
- What does he or she want most out of life?
- What is the person's greatest fear, worry, or problem now?
- Level of education and subjects of special interest
- Relationship to other family (parents, siblings, children, spouses)—include major changes, crises, disruptions, reconciliations
- How would the subject of the sermon impinge on this person's concerns?

At least one thing can be said for sure: if you complete such a case study, and then build a sermon which that person would understand, profit from, and participate in, your worries about being "relevant," clear, and direct are over. In fact, a concern for persons at the receiving end will have replaced anxiety over style and rhetoric, and that is the beginning of good preaching.

Chapter 21. **Preserving Historic Sites: Embarrassment Becoming Opportunity**

It is said that each profession has its characteristic vocational sin. For the ministry, it is plagiarism in the pulpit. Most of our laypeople and a good many honest and hard-working preachers do not know it, but an alarming number of sermons preached every Sunday morning did not come from the pens of the preachers delivering them. The pathetic thing is that much pulpit plagiarism is a very poor solution to a very real problem that *could* be handled differently and turned into an opportunity. That is the purpose and point of this chapter.

First, though, what is plagiarism? Debate can rage about when the fine line is crossed between the use of a source and plagiarism. On the whole, the key factor is the presence or absence of acknowledgment of the source's origins if they are other than the immediate author. Presumably a student who copied an entire term paper verbatim from a journal article and properly footnoted it might flunk the course on educational grounds, but would not be guilty of plagiarism. What we are talking about now are the unacknowledged uses of other people's material—in a word, stealing it.

In the pulpit that sometimes consists of using a whole sermon, sometimes of using several pieces of other sermons hooked together. Sometimes an illustration or even a novel idea is taken over from another source so completely that it must be considered plagiarized, even though a simple, "A great preacher once reminded us. . . ." would neutralize the moral stigma, as would a bulletin note giving credit where it is due. It certainly has to be said, though incredibly enough many preachers do not want to agree, that what would be plagiarism in a piece of writing is also plagiarism when that writing is delivered orally.

Why, one has to ask, would an otherwise honorable preacher stoop to stealing someone else's sermon? Maybe there was no time to prepare an original sermon, maybe catastrophe intervened, maybe the cartoon pinned up on my office door really happened—it shows a preacher leaning over the pulpit to say, "Due to a heavy schedule of weddings, workshops, and funerals this week, I haven't had time to prepare a sermon, so if somebody will kindly toss out a few human frailties, sins, and what have you, I'll wing it."[1] But *that* would at least have been an honest approach!

The preacher's weekly task is, of course, enormous, taken on the whole. Assuming that an average preacher is in the pulpit each week of the year except for study leaves and vacations, and that he or she will reuse each of the sermons prepared for those weeks periodically in different parishes, that still leaves a sizable sermon "barrel" to be filled: conservatively estimated, 460 sermons, or enough manuscript to print up into twenty books the size of this one. A conscientious preacher who disdains reusing sermons even in new preaching situations can in the course of a career write a couple of thousand sermons. The very idea that preachers, who on the whole are a fairly representative slice of the population in terms of background, ability, and energy, could routinely produce that much original thought and commentary is to say the least mind-boggling. At the same time that we deplore plagiarism, we ought at least to allow a moment's admiration for the honest preachers who turn to the task faithfully and scrupulously, in and out of the seasons of life that assail them as surely as they do the unordained!

But sympathy for the preacher's task does not excuse plagiarism. Even if it were not to be condemned on moral grounds, it would fall just as hard on psychological ones. At least unconsciously, lying to people is communicated and erodes relationships as surely as though the crime were in full view. The reason good psychotherapists do not ever lie to their patients, for instance, is not only because it is morally wrong, but even more importantly because lying inexorably eats away at the therapeutic relationship creating a misalliance rather than a healing bond, *even though the process is entirely unconscious to the client.* The same is true for the special pastor-people relationship that is always established, whatever its quality, in preaching.

We are still, however, faced with the enormity of the preaching task. There is something else we are faced with that is not usually talked about, but enters the rather bleak picture just here. Most people do not regularly hear more than a handful of preachers in their lifetimes, and most of those preachers are the faithful bedrock of ministry, but not pulpit greats by a long shot. The question arises, would it not be a plus if there were some way of letting sermon hearers participate in some of the great preaching of history? If there were a way to do it, who among us would turn down the opportunity for our people to hear a Fosdick or a Scherer or a Buttrick; to listen again (even if in disagreement) to a Peter Marshall; to sample the formative preaching of Jonathan Edwards or Timothy Dwight, the agonized faithfulness of Bonhoeffer or Niemöller, or even for that matter the insightfulness of our contemporaries whom no one except their people knows?

One begins to wonder, and then to worry, about the lost riches of great sermons preached once or twice, perhaps published and read by a few, but for the most part fallen silent soon after their creation. What would we say about the stewardship of human resources and creativity from that angle? One of the most significant sermons ever preached in the tumultuous days of the 1960s, I am convinced, was heard by an original congregation of fewer than 300 people in a college chapel service.[2] The preacher was murdered not long thereafter; the sermon was never published, and the copy I possess was sent me as a favor by its author soon after delivery. For all I know, it may be one of the few copies extant. Multiplied by the thousands, that is a haunting fact to reflect on.

Thoughts such as these led to the development of a seminary

course that had this objective: *teach preachers how to use other preachers' sermons honestly and creatively as an appropriate tool for ministry.* The basic idea is simplicity itself: a preacher announces that on a given Sunday he or she will be delivering the sermon of a certain other preacher (having secured necessary permission, of course, in conformity with copyright laws). An explanatory note about the original author and the circumstances of the sermon (if known) is printed in the Sunday bulletin. The preacher delivers the sermon using the best interpretative skills he or she can muster, and it is offered openly to the congregation as an opportunity for them to hear a "preacher" and a sermon they would otherwise never be exposed to. Instead of plagiarism, we have a unique teaching opportunity. *The only thing standing between plagiarism and using other sermons responsibly and creatively is acknowledgment.* Perhaps the real shame of plagiarism is that it is so easy not only to avoid but also to transform into a uniquely valuable preaching experience.

Great or historic sermons can be used, either singly or in series. For example, a series of four such "other voices" sermons preached every other week in the summer could all be examples of "pastoral preaching" or all different approaches to the same text or theme. Or a series of sermons representing different eras in the history of the church could be constructed: Augustine (who "preaches" surprisingly well in modern English) or Chrysostom from the early church, Calvin or Luther from the Reformation, Jonathan Edwards or Cotton Mather from Puritan America, Paul Scherer or Harry Emerson Fosdick from modern times. The possibilities are vast and readily available through printed collections of sermons.[3]

There are three essential ingredients to this use of historic sermons. The first has been mentioned: providing full and scrupulous information about the author and sermon, for teaching as well as proper acknowledgment purposes. The second ingredient is beyond the scope of this book: good oral interpretation. The sermon should be *delivered,* not just read. If a preacher needs help developing knowledge and skills of oral interpretation, there are probably local resources available: the speech departments and teachers of a nearby college or secondary school if not a seminary. For that matter, practically every town no matter how small contains *someone* who is trained to read well aloud and could be enlisted as a tutor. (Fundamentally, of course, a preacher should get that kind of continuing education help anyway, whether historic sermons are used or not. The effective interpretation of scripture—not dramatic acting—is probably one of the least developed but most useful and appreciated communication skills of ministry.) The goal in delivering a historic sermon is for it to have that conversational sense of what a speech colleague calls "first-timeness" rather than the feeling of a written piece being read aloud.

The third essential part of using historic sermons calls for some explanation. Such sermons must almost always be edited to make them shorter. Only within the past few years have American congregations and preachers grown accustomed to sermons about twenty minutes long. Let them go to thirty—or forty, heaven forbid—and practically everyone will squirm, even though until fairly recently a forty-minute sermon was mostly the norm. Concretely, that means that most preaching we will be using as historic sermons is too long to begin with. They need to be edited, sometimes to remove as much as 50 percent of the content.

Can that be done without hopelessly mutilating an otherwise good, even great, sermon? Yes. We call on an old editor's insight: a good piece of writing can almost always be edited for brevity; a bad one cannot. Presumably that is because good writing has at its foundation a clarity of purpose, thought, and expression that, like the basic branch structure of a tree, survives careful pruning without losing its identity or effectiveness. It may be, for instance, that the original uses two illustrations where one would do; or perhaps an aside from the main development can be omitted without damage. Editing should be done not only, or even primarily, by cutting out whole paragraphs, but also by trimming sentences within paragraphs or even, occasionally, phrases within sentences. The original sermon most likely is longer not so much because it had more to say as that it had more time for the elaboration of a basic thought or narrative development that we would compress into twenty minutes—and can still effectively do with sensitive but firm editing.

If, by chance, at the beginning of this discussion the historic sermon method had some initial appeal as a time saver over preparing original sermons, it should by now have lost it. The time investment required for selecting, announcing, editing, and practicing interpretation of someone else's sermon will likely be as much as for one's own. What is different is the kind of energy put to the task, and the kind of communication experience that results. If a preacher is "too busy" or otherwise unable to prepare an original sermon or to edit a historic one for use in this way, then it is surely time for him or her to ask some serious vocational questions about the preaching ministry. A book appeared some years ago with a variation on the historic sermon idea, offered as a *time saver* for preachers. That is absurd.

In order to edit well you have, for instance, to know the sermon so well that you almost are thinking like the original author—conscious of the sermon's basic purpose and structure, knowing the difference between what is elaboration and what moves us a step forward, what is redundancy of expression and what is adding new information, what is contextual but less meaningful today, and what is timeless. You will have to get thoroughly enough into the sermon and its own expression to be able to decide, if need be, to leave some of the conceptualization behind without doing violence to either the purpose or the style of the original. (One of the nice by-products of this approach in the seminary course was that students discovered the editing experience to be an education in itself both in how to develop sermons and in how to think theologically in the operational pressure of preaching. Realizing that choosing to omit a sentence is at base a *theological* decision as much if not more than a literary one is a form of theological education we can never get too much of.)

Showing is probably better than telling about editing. On the following page is reproduced a page of text (Fig. 1) from one of the most famous and moving sermons of all time, Arthur John Gossip's "But When Life Tumbles In, What Then?"—the first sermon preached after Gossip's wife suddenly died.[4] It has every bit as much if not more power to move and heal today as it did when first preached. Unfortunately, it would run better than forty-five minutes preached today in its original form. Figure 2 shows how the page we are sampling is reduced by virtually half, giving us the result shown in Figure 3. Read the original page aloud, and then read the edited page aloud. It becomes clear that the sermon as a piece of creative work from the hand of a master preacher is basically intact; it has been edited, not slaughtered.

Experience in teaching editing to seminary students is quite encouraging. Most get the hang of editing quickly and easily, once they have gotten over their initial reluctance to edit *within paragraphs and sentences* rather than simply to omit paragraphs here and there. The middle sentence of one paragraph may be reconnected to the third of another one following, with intervening sentences edited out; or the second half of a long, compound sentence may be cut out and the thought taken up by the next complete sentence. Students learning to do that also quickly become aware of their own theological investments showing in the editing process. When you ask yourself *why* you would cut this paragraph but not the next one, the answer may prove to be merely technical; but it may also prove to be theological at its core.

Once the editing task is done, one important preparatory step remains in the writing stage: making the preaching manuscript. Surprisingly, even that simple-seeming chore has its complexities. For instance, one should not type a manuscript using all capital letters on the assumption that being bigger

Figure 1

life was not to give what you expected from it, that your dreams were not to be granted, that yours was to be a steep and lonely road, that some tremendous sacrifice was to be asked of you, could you make shift to face it with a shadow of the Master's courage and the Master's calm? For there is no supposing in the matter. To a certainty to you too, in your turn, some day, these things must come.

[2] Yes, unbelievably they come. For years and years you and I go our sunny way and live our happy lives, and the rumors of these terrors are blown to us very faintly as from a world so distant that it seems to have nothing to do with us; and then, to us too, it happens. And when it does, nobody has the right to snivel or whimper as if something unique and inexplicable had befallen him. "Never morning wore to evening but some heart did break"—hearts just as sensitive as yours and mine. But when yours breaks, what then? It is a bit late in the day to be talking about insurance when one's house is ablaze from end to end: and somewhat tardy to be searching for something to bring one through when the test is upon one. And how are you and I, so querulous and easily fretted by the minor worries, to make shift at all in the swelling of Jordan, with the cold of it catching away our breath, and the rush of it plucking at our footing?

[3] Goethe, of course, tells us that all the religions were designed to meet us and to give us help, just there; to enable us to bear the unbearable, to face the impossible, to see through with some kind of decency and honour what obviously can't be done at all.

[4] But then so many people's religion is a fair-weather affair. A little rain, and it runs and crumbles; a touch of strain, and it snaps. How often out at the front one lay and watched an aeroplane high up in the blue and sunlight, a shimmering, glistening, beautiful thing: and then there came one shot out of a cloud, and it crashed down to earth, a broken mass of twisted metal. And many a one's religion is like that. So long as God's will runs parallel to ours, we follow blithely. But the moment that they cross, or clash, that life grows difficult, that we don't understand, how apt faith is to fail us just when we have most need of it! You remember our Lord's story of the two men who lived in the same village, and went to the same synagogue, and sat in the same pew, listening to the same services: and how one day some kind of gale blew into their lives, a fearsome storm. And in the one case, everything collapsed, and for a moment there were some poor spars tossing upon wild waters, and then, nothing at all. For that unhappy soul had built on sand, and in his day of need, everything was undermined, and vanished. But the other, though he too had to face the emptiness, the loneliness, the pain, came through it all braver and stronger and mellower and nearer God. For he had built upon the rock. Well, what of you and me? We have found it a business to march with the infantry, how will we keep up with the horsemen: if the small ills of life have frayed our faith and temper, what will we do in the roar and black swirl of Jordan?

[5] That has always been my chief difficulty about preaching. Carlyle, you recall, used to say that the chirpy optimism of Emerson maddened him,

Figure 2

life was not to give what you expected from it, that your dreams were not to be granted, that yours was to be a steep and lonely road, that some tremendous sacrifice was to be asked of you, could you make shift to face it with a shadow of the Master's courage and the Master's calm? For there is no supposing in the matter. To a certainty to you too, in your turn, some day, these things must come.

~~² Yes, unbelievably they come. For years and years you and I go our sunny way and live our happy lives, and the rumors of these terrors are blown to us very faintly as from a world so distant that it seems to have nothing to do with us; and then, to us too, it happens. And when it does, nobody has the right to snivel or whimper as if something unique and inexplicable had befallen him.~~ "Never morning wore to evening but some heart did break"—hearts just as sensitive as yours and mine. But when yours breaks, what then? ~~It is a bit late in the day to be talking about insurance when one's house is ablaze from end to end: and somewhat tardy to be searching for something to bring one through when the test is upon one. And~~ how are you and I, so querulous and easily fretted by the minor worries, to make shift at all in the swelling of Jordan, with the cold of it catching away our breath, and the rush of it plucking at our footing?

~~³ Goethe, of course, tells us that all the religions were designed to meet us and to give us help, just there; to enable us to bear the unbearable, to face the impossible, to see through with some kind of decency and honour what obviously can't be done at all.~~

~~⁴ But then~~ so many people's religion is a fair-weather affair. A little rain, and it runs and crumbles; a touch of strain, and it snaps. ~~How often out at the front one lay and watched an aeroplane high up in the blue and sunlight, a shimmering, glistening, beautiful thing: and then there came one shot out of a cloud, and it crashed down to earth, a broken mass of twisted metal. And many a one's religion is like that.~~ So long as God's will runs parallel to ours, we follow blithely. But the moment that they cross, or clash, that life grows difficult, that we don't understand, how apt faith is to fail us just when we have most need of it! ~~You remember our Lord's story of the two men who lived in the same village, and went to the same synagogue, and sat in the same pew, listening to the same services: and how one day some kind of gale blew into their lives, a fearsome storm. And in the one case, everything collapsed, and for a moment there were some poor spars tossing upon wild waters, and then, nothing at all. For that unhappy soul had built on sand, and in his day of need, everything was undermined, and vanished. But the other, though he too had to face the emptiness, the loneliness, the pain, came through it all braver and stronger and mellower and nearer God. For he had built upon the rock.~~ Well, what of you and me? We have found it a business to march with the infantry, how will we keep up with the horsemen: if the small ills of life have frayed our faith and temper, what will we do in the roar and black swirl of Jordan?

~~⁵ That has always been my chief difficulty about preaching. Carlyle, you recall, used to say that the chirpy optimism of Emerson maddened him,~~

Figure 3

... life was not to give you what you expected from it, that your dreams were not to be granted, that yours was to be a steep and lonely road, that some tremendous sacrifice was to be asked of you, could you make shift to face it with a shadow of the Master's courage and the Master's calm? For there is no supposing in the matter. To a certainty to you too, in your turn, some day, these things must come.

"Never morning wore to evening but some heart did break"—hearts just as sensitive as yours and mine. But when yours breaks, what then? How are you and I, so querulous and easily fretted by the minor worries, to make shift at all in the swelling of Jordan, with the cold of it catching away our breath, and the rush of it plucking at our footing?

So many people's religion is a fair-weather affair. A little rain, and it runs and crumbles; a touch of strain, and it snaps. So long as God's will runs parallel to ours, we follow blithely. But the moment that they cross, or clash, that life grows difficult, that we don't understand, how apt faith is to fail us just when we have most need of it! Well, what of you and me? We have found it a busines to march with the infantry, how will we keep up with the horsemen: if the small ills of life have frayed our faith and temper, what will we do in the roar and black swirl of Jordan?

they will be easier to read. Quite the contrary, since we are used to reading upper- and lower-case type, a line of all capitals is actually *harder* for the eye and brain to read, no matter what the size. Stick with regular upper- and lower-case typing. If you have access to a large-type typewriter, fine, but it is not really necessary.

TO TEST THE DIFFERENCE, THIS PARAGRAPH IS A REPETITION OF PART OF THE ONE BEFORE. FOR IN-STANCE, ONE SHOULD NOT TYPE A MANUSCRIPT US-ING ALL CAPITAL LETTERS ON THE ASSUMPTION THAT BEING BIGGER THEY WILL BE EASIER TO READ. QUITE THE CONTRARY, SINCE WE ARE USED TO READ-ING UPPER- AND LOWER-CASE TYPE, A LINE OF ALL CAPITALS IS ACTUALLY HARDER FOR THE EYE AND BRAIN TO READ, NO MATTER WHAT THE SIZE.

The page size and layout of a preaching manuscript (whether your own or someone else's sermon) is equally important. Using half-pages turned end-wise with double-spaced typing gives a book-sized reading surface that is far easier to read from than a whole, letter-sized sheet with typing all the way across. The reason is simple: normal eyesight can take in a width of about 5 inches on one "shot" or movement of the eye. That is one line, or paragraph, on the half-page manuscript. A longer line will require two or more "fixes" of the eye, and although they happen in micromilliseconds they are poisonous to the "first time" sense of "prepared conversation," as my colleague William Brower puts it, including the eye contact that good manu-script delivery aims for.[5] The properly prepared delivery of a sermon from a manuscript will give no clue to the listening people that anything but perhaps a few notes is being used to prompt the preacher. If you are more dependent than that on a manuscript during delivery, either you do not know the ser-mon well enough or the manuscript itself is inadequately repro-duced. (Here, however, is the place to sound a warning against memorizing a sermon and giving it without note or manuscript. The underlying and perhaps unconscious anxiety of forgetting one's lines communicates so successfully despite a preacher's best intentions that most such occasions are exercises in suspense rather than sharing the good news. Anyone can commit a piece to memory and recite it; most of us can learn to interpret in reading so that it souunds fresh; but few indeed can deliver a memorized line so successfully and so free from anxiety that it sounds spontaneous. And most of those people are highly paid and praised actors, not preachers.)

It will prove helpful to tinker with the physical layout of the pulpit manuscript in two further ways. For one thing, separate each double spaced paragraph by a triple space, so that each paragraph is a visual "clump" of print for the eye to get hold of. Make paragraphs for length rather than for sense, by the way, for delivery purposes. More than half a dozen or so lines of type is too much and calls for a new, triple-spaced, paragraph division. The other thing is to go through and underline key words in a stand-out color ink, perhaps to the extent of two words per line. Your manuscript *for delivery* looks like Figure 4, which is an approximation of these typing guidelines with somewhat shorter lines because of the limits of the book page.

While it pays to watch out for details such as making a manuscript, we should not lose sight of the objective of the whole process: to provide an opportunity for preachers to rest a bit with integrity from their own creative labors and to offer their people an opportunity to experience a broader scope of preaching than they otherwise would be able to. A few stalwart converts to the historic sermon system, growing out of the seminary course that launched the idea, report considerable enthusiasm for the whole process. One preacher devotes one Sunday every month or so to a historic sermon, and his people feel not only stimulated by the variety but also included as partners in the preaching task in ways not otherwise experienced. The only sorry thing is that the idea had to grow out of such a negative beginning as a counteractive for pulpit plagiarism. With this tool at hand, though, the plagiarist has no room for cover, and that is as it should be.

Figure 4

    <u>Suppose</u> that to <u>you</u>, as to <u>Christ</u>, it became evident that <u>life</u> was not to give what you <u>expected</u> from it, that your <u>dreams</u> were not to be <u>granted</u>, that yours was to be a <u>steep</u> and <u>lonely</u> road, that some tremendous <u>sacrifice</u> was to be <u>asked</u> of you, could you <u>make</u> the <u>shift</u> to <u>face</u> it with a <u>shadow</u> of the Master's <u>courage</u> and the Master's <u>calm</u>?

    For there is <u>no supposing</u> in the matter. To a certainty to you too, in your <u>turn</u>, some day, these things must <u>come</u>. "Never <u>morning</u> wore to evening but some <u>heart</u> did break"--hearts just as <u>sensitive</u> as yours and mine.

Figure 4—*Continued*

But when yours breaks, what then?

And how are you and I, so querulous and easily fretted by the minor worries, to make shift at all in the swelling Jordan, with the cold of it catching away our breath, and the rush of it plucking at our footing?

So many people's religion is a fair-weather affair. A little rain, and it runs and crumbles; a touch of strain, and it snaps. So long as God's will runs parallel to ours, we follow blithely. But the moment that they cross, or clash, that life grows difficult, that we don't understand, how apt faith is to fail us just when we have most need of it!

Chapter 22. **Consumer Protection: A Bill of Rights for Congregations**

Working throughout this book has been a hopeful premise that now, at the end, can have a place of its own.[1] The idea has been that communication through preaching is by its nature a shared enterprise between preacher and listener, an undertaking to which the listener brings energy, commitment, and a willingness to participate. It would perhaps not be necessary to say that so directly were not so much of our homiletics built on the unstated assumption that preachers have to struggle with their people to be appreciated, understood, or believed. There is a lot of struggle in preaching, to be sure; part of the burden of this book has been to encourage preachers to use that struggle in their preaching itself. It is quite a different thing, however, for preaching to become a kind of adversarial process between preacher and congregation.

A line in one of W. E. Orchard's prayers reads, "So often we pray for that which is already ours, neglected and unappropriated; so often for that which never can be ours; so often for that which we must win ourselves."[2] Perhaps our thinking and worrying about preaching has sometimes got itself backward in somewhat the same ways.

I have often noticed preachers struggling to induce or manufacture certain kinds of congregational participation and response that, honestly, the congregation members were willing and ready to give without effort if only they were allowed the chance. Perhaps we have underrated them in certain key areas, which the following "Bill of Rights" tries to spotlight. My underlying principle is this: human beings for the most part do not need to be *taught* to communicate; they do need to be *allowed* to. Here then is a summary of much of what we have been saying in these pages.

1. *Give your people credit for recognizing and prizing imagination in preaching, no matter how experimental the message form.* To the preacher who says people cannot appreciate the finest fruits of his or her imagination, I have to ask, first, whether the fruit is ripe enough to eat, and second, whether a good selection has been offered them lately.

2. *Give your people credit for empathizing with the preacher who truly struggles with the sermon and for valuing that struggle no matter what the outcome.* For example, the preacher who confesses to his or her people, "I haven't finished this sermon because I honestly don't have any final answers, and I'm still struggling with it" will, I suspect, find an eager participation in the struggle rather than the rejection feared for not having produced a finished masterpeice.

3. *Give your people credit for wanting to share the biblical experience, but not to worship it or bow reflexively to its authority.* It can be a homiletical revelation to discover that biblical contents are neither *kerygma* nor *didache* but first and foremost reflections on lived religious experience. Call them "residues" of dramatically changed understanding and living, attempts to share episodes of religious growth and perception—and the Bible suddenly comes alive. The Bible is neither to be "believed" nor "revered" but rather to be *joined.*

4. *Give your people credit for seeking consciously and actively a personal connection between their life situations and the words you are saying.* I am worried about the preacher who struggles to create bridges of relevance between sermon and people and who worries endlessly about "reaching" people and "involving" them with what he or she is saying. If a preacher is truly sharing a congregation's life and struggle, then tuning into his or her own needs is a fair place to start getting in touch with the congregation's struggles. The homiletical question ought to be, "What do I want to say to and for myself?"

5. *Give your people credit for appreciating being allowed to share the dynamics of sermon preparation itself, even if the message is not as smooth and finished as you would like.* Amazingly, many preachers never

hint that their messages have come out of all kinds of study, conversation, false starts, fragments of experience, and a fair amount of anxiety. I have often found that telling people what I started out wanting to say, and what difficulties and opportunities I encountered along the road of creating a message to say it, was itself as good a sermon as I could have wanted. There is an educator's rule of thumb at work here: once you have made clear to students what the objective of your teaching is, most of your teaching has already been done.

6. *Give your people credit for sharing, forgiving, and even growing from the homiletical duds that you preach.* Perhaps a surgeon cannot afford to relax about failures, but surely a preacher can. I believe I have gotten closer to many sermon hearers by confessing, and even laughing about, sermons that fizzled than by receiving their praise for those that soared. The sermon that failed may also communicate an essential message in its own peculiar way, leading to the response from a congregation, "If the preacher has trouble with that idea (or text, or problem, or incident) too, I don't feel quite so alone out here."

7. *Give your people credit for being open to conflict and controversy in preaching, perhaps more so than you are yourself.* The great emotional, social, and developmental issues of human growth and relationship are in one way or another conflict management issues. It is hard to see how preaching that does *not* relate to the growth conflicts of people's lives can be preaching "where the people are."

8. *Give your people credit for being able both to enjoy and benefit from a sermon.* It is depressing how many people feel guilty when they actually enjoy and are entertained by a sermon. It is just as depressing to hear sermons in which it is painfully obvious that the preacher has made an almost conscious effort to purge the message of any lightness, intrigue, narrative interest, or linguistic color. A preacher would do well to keep in mind that some of the most effective communication in human history has come from the age-old figure of the storyteller, whose product was enjoyable before it was anything else.

9. *Give your people credit for perceiving and valuing the connections, theme, and wholeness among sermon and other elements of worship.* A preacher loses a lot of communication energy if he or she assumes that the message starts or stops with the sermon itself. It is not even too much to rely on such worship elements as calls to worship, confessions, hymns, scripture (of course), and prayers to carry much of the message of the sermon, especially in introductory and concluding ways. People *do* make those connections and are well able without much prompting on the preacher's part to perceive the worship experience as a total message.

10. *Give your people credit for wanting to learn the language of religious experience and expression.* The dynamics of religious language in theory have to do with expressing deep feelings, needs, and convictions beyond the realm of ordinary description. In practice, that means that religious language used by the preacher appropriate to its expressive dynamic is *not* something alien to the people. Theological language applied descriptively or metaphysically is another matter, and some would say that such talk is alien not only to congregations but also to theology. Preachers who worry that their people will be afraid of God-talk or unresponsive to it may not be probing deeply enough into either the work of language or the felt needs people have to communicate and interpret their deepest experiences.

Allowing people to participate in communication may indeed take some hard work—to help them be free from rigid patterns, to support them in expressing difficult or tabooed thoughts and feelings, or to encourage their searching for new and different ways of expression. But the tide is running *with* communication, not against it. The Communication Bill of Rights is simply an attempt to chart the current and to encourage preachers to get over what for some is a morbid fear that anything natural and positive about preaching must be wrong.

Notes

Chapter 1

1. Fitzhugh Dodson, *How to Parent* (New York: New American Library), p. 234.
2. Harry Emerson Fosdick, *The Living of These Days* (New York: Harper & Row, 1956), p. 92.
3. Clement Welsh, *Preaching in a New Key: Studies in the Psychology of Thinking and Listening* (Philadelphia: Pilgrim Press, 1974), pp. 15–16.
4. John Fry, "On Taking Charge of Your Own Experience," The Westervelt Lectures, Austin Presbyterian Theological Seminary, Austin, Texas, 1974.
5. For a good overview, see Ernest R. Hilgard and Gordon H. Bower, eds., *Theories of Learning*, 3rd ed. (New York: Appleton-Century-Crofts, 1966).
6. See especially R. P. Abelson et al., eds., *Theories of Cognitive Consistency* (Chicago: Rand-McNally, 1969); and D. E. Berlyne, *Conflict, Arousal and Curiosity* (New York: McGraw-Hill, 1960).
7. Harold M. Schroder, Michael J. Driver, and Siegfried Streufort, *Human Information Processing: Individuals and Groups Functioning in Complex Social Situations* (New York: Holt, Rinehart and Winston, 1967), p. 36, e.g.
8. Karl Barth, *The Word of God and the Word of Man*, trans. Douglas Horton (New York: Harper & Brothers, 1957), p. 100.
9. Ulrich Simon, *Theology of Crisis* (London: S.P.C.K., 1948), p. 187.

Chapter 2

1. Viktor E. Frankl, *Man's Search for Meaning* (New York: Washington Square Press, 1963), pp. 139–40.
2. William Muehl, *All the Damned Angels* (Philadelphia: Pilgrim Press, 1972), p. 39.
3. Simon, *Theology of Crisis*, p. 15.

Chapter 3

1. Karl Barth, *Church Dogmatics* I/2, trans. G. T. Thomson and Harold Knight (Edinburgh: T. & T. Clark, 1960), p. 746.
2. Krister Stendahl, "Paul and the Introspective Conscience of the West," *Harvard Theological Review* 56 (July 1963): 199–215.
3. For an insightful discussion of the concept of love *vís-a-vís* aggression in Christian perspective, see Seward Hiltner, "A Theological Note on Aggression," in Sydney Smith, ed., *The Human Mind Revisited: Essays in Honor of Karl A. Menninger* (New York: International Universities Press, 1978), pp. 205–13.
4. Paul E. Scherer, *The Word God Sent* (New York: Harper & Row, 1965), p. 242.
5. Seward Hiltner, "Salvation's Message About Health," address to the Consultation on Health and Salvation, World Council of Churches, Tübingen, Germany, 1 September 1967.
6. James Barr, *The Semantics of Biblical Language* (London: Oxford University Press, 1961), pp. 215–17.
7. Hiltner, "A Theological Note on Aggression."

Chapter 4

1. George Gerbner, "An Institutional Approach to Mass Communications Research," in Lee Thayer, ed., *Communication: Theory and Research*, (Springfield, Ill.: Charles C. Thomas, 1967), pp. 430–51.
2. Martin E. P. Seligman, *Helplessness: On Depression, Development, and Death* (San Francisco: W. H. Freeman, 1975).
3. Sheldon Kopp, *An End to Innocence* (New York: Macmillan, 1978), p. 12. The term "pseudoinnocence" is attributed to Rollo May.

Chapter 5

1. Victor Turner, *Dramas, Fields, and Metaphors: Symbolic Action in Human Society* (Ithaca: Cornell University Press, 1974). See also an earlier version of his essay, by the same title, "Passages, Margins, and Poverty: Religious Symbols of Communitas," *Worship* 46, no. 7 (August/September 1972): 390–412.
2. Charles Rhind Joy, *Harper's Topical Concordance*, rev. ed. (New York: Harper & Row, 1961).

Chapter 6

1. James D. Smart, *The Strange Silence of the Bible in the Church* (Philadelphia: Westminster Press, 1970); also J. Stanley Glen, *The Recovery of the Teaching Ministry* (Philadelphia: Westminster Press, 1960).
2. See, for instance, Harold Rugg, *Imagination: An Inquiry into the Sources and Conditions That Stimulate Creativity* (New York: Harper & Row, 1963); James E. Loder, *Religious Pathology and Christian Faith* (Philadelphia: Westminster Press, 1966); and Frank Barron, "The Psychology of Creativity," in *New Directions in Psychology II* (New York: Holt, Rinehart and Winston, 1965).

Chapter 7

1. Richard Hofstadter, *Anti-Intellectualism in American Life* (New York: Knopf, 1963).

2. Jean Piaget, *The Language and Thought of the Child*, trans. Marjorie Gabain (Cleveland: World, 1955).

3. Kopp, *An End to Innocence*.

4. J. Randall Nichols, *Conflict and Creativity: The Dynamics of the Communication Process in Theological Perspective*, unpublished doctoral dissertation, Princeton Theological Seminary, 1970.

5. Driver, Schroder and Streufort, *Human Information Processing*.

Chapter 8

1. Bernard Martin, *If God Does Not Die*, trans. James H. Farley (Richmond, Va.: John Knox Press, 1966), p. 63.

2. H. H. Farmer, *The Servant of the Word* (New York: Scribner's, 1942), *Preacher's Paperback Library* edition, p. 16.

3. Seward Hiltner, "The Minister in the Human Circus," *Pastoral Psychology* 22, no. 219 (December 1971): 13–20.

Chapter 9

1. James E. Dittes, *The Church in the Way* (New York: Scribner's, 1967).

2. Harry Emerson Fosdick, *The Hope of the World* (New York: Harper & Brothers, 1933).

Chapter 10

1. George A. Miller, "The Magical Number Seven, Plus or Minus Two" in Donald C. Hildum, ed., *Language and Thought* (Princeton, N.J.: D. Van Nostrand, 1967), pp. 3–32.

2. Michael Novak, *Ascent of the Mountain, Flight of the Dove: An Invitation to Religious Studies* (New York: Harper & Row, 1971).

3. Conrad Harry Massa, "Preaching as Confluence," Inaugural Lecture, Princeton Theological Seminary, Princeton, New Jersey, 6 December 1978.

4. D. Campbell Wyckoff, *Theory and Design of Christian Education Curriculum* (Philadelphia: Westminster Press, 1961), p. 17 *et passim*.

Chapter 11

1. This and the following chapter appeared as "The Languages of Preaching" in *The Military Chaplain's Review*, Fall 1975, pp. 13–25.

2. Brendan Maher, "Language and Psychopathology," in George A. Miller, ed., *Communication, Language and Meaning: Psychological Perspectives* (New York: Basic Books, 1973).

3. Howard Gardner, *The Quest for Mind* (New York: Vintage Books, 1974), p. 66.

4. Ian T. Ramsey, *Religious Language: An Empirical Placing of Theological Phrases* (New York: Macmillan, 1957).

5. Paul Ricoeur, "Biblical Hermeneutics, *Semeia* 4 (1975): 78.

6. Coming from Piaget's work, the idea is discussed by John H. Flavell, *The Developmental Psychology of Jean Piaget* (Princeton, N.J.: D. Van Nostrand, 1963), pp. 151–55, in regard to the emergence of the symbolic function in children. The same idea, using Piaget's original term "nominal realism," is discussed by Hans G. Furth, *Piaget and Knowledge* (Englewood Cliffs, N.J.:

Prentice-Hall, 1969), pp. 111–12. The original discussion is to be found in Jean Piaget, *Play, Dreams and Imitation in Childhood,* trans. C. Gattengo and F. M. Hodgson (New York: Norton, 1962).
7. Gilkey, *Naming the Whirlwind,* pp. 260, 419.

Chapter 12

1. J. Randall Nichols, "Notes Toward a Theological View of Responsibility in Communication," *Explorations in Communication III* 3, no. 1 (1978): 125 ff.
2. Piaget, *Play, Dreams and Imitation in Childhood,* p. 273; see also my application of Piagetian theory to the communication process in Nichols, *Conflict and Creativity,* pp. 195–99, 400–404.
3. Maher, "Language and Psychopathology," p. 258.
4. Ibid., p. 260.
5. Gilkey, *Naming the Whirlwind.*

Chapter 13

1. This chapter originally appeared as "Ministry and Diagnosis: Teaching Ministers to Guide Assessment and Evaluation in Personal, Congregational, and Community Life," paper presented to the Association for Professional Education for Ministry, Toronto, Ontario, June 1978, and printed in their proceedings that year, *Education for Ministry,* ed. Gaylord B. Noyce, pp. 82–87.
2. Dean M. Kelley, *Why Conservative Churches Are Growing: A Study in Sociology of Religion* (New York: Harper & Row, 1972).
3. Paul W. Pruyser, *The Minister as Diagnostician* (Philadelphia: Westminster Press, 1976).
4. See, for example, Hiltner, "Towards Autonomous Pastoral Diagnosis," *Bulletin of the Menninger Clinic* 40, no. 5 (September 1976): 537–92; Don S. Browning, *The Moral Context of Pastoral Care* (Philadelphia: Westminster Press, 1976); and Karl A. Menninger, *Whatever Became of Sin?* (New York: Hawthorn Books, 1973).

Chapter 14

1. Phillips Brooks, *On Preaching* (New York: Seabury Press, 1964).
2. John Ryland Scotford, "A New Approach to the Teaching of Homiletics," *Journal of Religion* 7 (1927): 72–73.

Chapter 15

1. Barth, *Church Dogmatics,* I/2, pp. 744–46.

Chapter 17

1. Jean-Jacques Von Allmen, *Preaching and Congregation,* trans. B. L. Nicholas (Richmond, Va.: John Knox Press, 1962).
2. William Stephenson, *The Play Theory of Mass Communication* (Chicago: The University of Chicago Press, 1967), especially Chapter 3. See also George Gerbner, "Mass Media and Human Communication Theory," in Frank E. X. Dance, ed., *Human Communication Theory: Original Essays* (New York: Holt, Rinehart and Winston, 1967), p. 45.

3. Gerbner, "Mass Media and Human Communication Theory," p. 53.

4. See Leon Festinger, *Conflict, Decision and Dissonance* (Stanford: Stanford University Press, 1964).

5. John Moody, *Homiletical Responses to the Angela Davis Grant*, unpublished master's thesis (theology), Princeton Theological Seminary, 1978.

Chapter 18

1. Portions of this chapter appeared in oral form in a *Thesis* cassette tape, "Power Planning for Relevant Worship," 7, no. 10 (November, 1976).

2. Diogenes Allen, *The Reasonableness of Faith* (Washington, D.C.: Corpus Books, 1968), pp. 5–6.

3. Gerbner, "An Institutional Approach to Mass Communications Research."

4. Rudolph Bultmann, "Points of Contact and Conflict," *Essays Philosophical and Theological* (New York: Macmillan, 1950), p. 135. See also James E. Sellers, *The Outsider and the Word of God: A Study in Christian Communication* (New York: Abingdon Press, 1961).

5. Gilkey, *Naming the Whirlwind*, pp. 419–420.

6. For discussions of the overall issue, see Sellers, *The Outsider and the Word of God*, and Nichols, *Conflict and Creativity*, chap. 8.

7. Barr, *The Semantics of Biblical Language*.

8. Attributed to M. V. C. Jeffreys in Eric Lord, "Relevance and Revelation in Religious Education," *Religious Education* 64 (January/February 1969): 24.

Chapter 20

1. Edmund Holt Linn, *Preaching as Counselling: The Unique Method of Harry Emerson Fosdick* (Valley Forge, Pa.: Judson Press, 1966), p. 15.

2. Two excellent statements of that theory are those by Ramsey, *Religious Language*, and by Stephen Crites, "The Narrative Quality of Experience," *Journal of the American Academy of Religion* 39, no. 3 (September 1971): 291–310.

3. Morton Wiener and Albert Mehrabian, *Language Within Language: Immediacy, A Channel in Verbal Communication* (New York: Appleton-Century-Crofts, 1968).

Chapter 21

1. *Better Homes and Gardens* 56, no. 3 (March 1978): 232. Copyright © Meredith Corporation, 1978. All rights reserved.

2. Robert W. Spike, "Yearning After a Transcendent Glory," sermon preached in Rollins Chapel, Dartmouth College, Hanover, New Hampshire, March, 1961.

3. See, for instance, Andrew W. Blackwood, *The Protestant Pulpit* (New York: Abingdon Press, 1947); also Clyde E. Fant, Jr., and William M. Pinson, Jr., eds., *20 Centuries of Great Preaching*, 13 vols. (Waco, Tex.: Word Books, 1971).

4. Printed in Blackwood, *The Protestant Pulpit*, p. 199. Reprinted from A. J. Gossip, "But When Life Tumbles In, What Then?" From *The Hero in thy Soul* (New York: Charles Scribner's Sons, 1929; Scotland: T. & T. Clark). Used by permission of Scribner's Sons and T. & T. Clark.

5. With thanks to my colleague William Brower, Princeton Theological Seminary, Princeton, New Jersey, for the phrases "first-timeness" and "prepared conversation."

Chapter 22

1. This chapter originally appeared in J. Randall Nichols, "What Should We Teach the Preacher?" *Military Chaplain's Review*, Spring 1974, pp. 28–31.
2. W. E. Orchard, in Harry Emerson Fosdick, *The Meaning of Prayer* (New York: Association Press, 1949), p. 112.

Index

Abstraction in preaching, 35–39, 46, 64, 68, 72
Acceptance, 63
Accommodation, 71
Acknowledgment of sources, 144–55
Adolescence, 79
Adversarial attitude, 46, 158
Advertisements, 108–9
Affirmation, 82, 84
Aggression, 15–17, 133
Ambiguity, 37, 45, 74, 83
Anger, 11, 17, 21, 30, 38, 49, 134
Answer system, 84
Anti-intellectualism, 36
Anxiety, 48, 55, 90, 105, 108, 143, 154, 159
Apocalyptic, 77
Application of sermons, 35, 36, 44
Appropriation: of gospel, 138; of messages, 71
Assuming listener's perspective, 64–65, 74
Assumptions: in language development, 62; in preaching, 56, 108, 135
Attentiveness, of listeners, 35–39, 102–3, 117
Attitude toward preaching, 98
Audio-visuals, 57
Augustine, St., 147
Authority: biblical, 64; pastoral, 6
Authoritarianism, 78, 84

Barr, James, 15, 29, 130
Barth, Karl, 6, 13, 26, 42, 95
Beliefs, 10, 18, 108. *See also* Values
Bible, 49, 69, 73, 97, 159; as hermeneutic, 97; language of, 58; use of, 40, 60, 68, 128
Body of message, 101, 104
Bonhoeffer, Dietrich, 146
Brooding, 3, 131
Brooks, Phillips, 90, 91
Brower, William, 154
Bulletins, for worship, 54, 105, 144
Bultmann, Rudolph, 127
Buttrick, George, 146

Calvin, Jean, 147
Case studies, 80, 86, 140–43
Categories of sermons, 136
Children, 3, 22, 62–63; language of, 66–68
Christology, 95
Chrysostom, St. John, 147
Church, 10, 78–79, 109; early, 77
Church year, 57, 119
Clarity, 8, 102, 143
Clown, preacher as, 43
Code, 63, 74, 126, 127
Cognitive development, 35, 37
Comfort, 12, 85, 92
Commentaries, biblical, 31–34, 56, 130
Commission, 13, 16, 133

Commitment, 9, 64, 99
Communication, analysis of, 18; breakdown, 89; connection in, 62; contract for, 99–106, 116, 132; dynamics, 96, 107–14, 117; environment, 42, 97, 99; in preaching, 58, 99; nonverbal, 58, 100; obstacles to, 129–30; process of, 6, 27, 36, 38, 39, 41, 42, 71, 89, 101, 113, 132; work of, 18, 106, 110
Community, 119; formation of, 106–14
Complexity, 8, 39, 121
Concepts, in thinking, 52; theological, 40, 44, 83, 86, 122, 123
Conclusions, of sermons, 96, 104
Concreteness, in sermons, 35–39
Conflict, 5, 9, 54, 110–11, 127, 160
Confrontation, in sermons, 134
Congregations, 45, 54, 55, 92, 99, 106–14, 119, 148, 158, 159, 160, 161. See also Community
Congruence, 61, 90, 134
Consciousness, expanding, 38
Context, for language, 61, 68, 69–75; of biblical text, 126
Continuing education, 48, 116
Conviction, 12–17, 60, 161
Counseling, pastoral, 41, 45, 67, 79, 101. See also Psychotherapy
Creation, 11, 72, 122
Creativity, 34, 78, 123, 133, 146
Crisis, 6, 7, 12, 135
Criteria, of preaching, 8, 36, 117
Crucifixion, 131
Cultivation, communication as, 108, 111, 122
Curriculum, in education, 56–57

Davis, Angela, 110–12
Death, 19
Decision, in preaching, 64, 108
Decontextualization, of language, 71–75
Delivery, of sermon, 147
Denial, of feelings, 134
Dependency, 18, 133
Depression, 19, 40, 60, 76, 133
Description, 63, 84, 123, 126, 161
Development, human, 41

Developmental psychology, 36, 61–62
Diagnosis, in preaching, 75–87
Diagnostician, 77
Dialectic, 7, 26, 27
Dialogue, hermeneutical, 40, 42
Didache, 159
Digestion of sermons, 94–98
Disciples, 84
Discipleship, 14, 60, 99, 133
Discipline, 120
Disclosure, 141
Discontinuity, 89
Discovery, 6, 93, 103
Dittes, James, 47
Dodson, Fitzhugh, 2
Doubt. See Uncertainty
Dwight, Timothy, 146

Easter, 110
Editing, of historic sermons, 148–52
Education, 35, 45, 64, 122, 159; Christian, 56, 57, 93; clinical-pastoral, 90; continuing 85, 86, 148; theological, 38, 76, 77, 86, 150
Edwards, Jonathan, 146–47
Effectiveness, communication, 64; in preaching, 46, 123
Eisegesis, 26–30, 55, 125
Empathy, 39, 158
Encounter, God-person, 42, 99, 141
Enjoyment, of sermons, 160
Ethics, 42, 81, 82
Evaluation, of sermons, 117
Exegesis, 26, 91
Expectations, in communication, 45, 99, 100–106
Experience, 3, 4, 27, 39, 52, 60, 72, 77, 104; and language, 61–68, 73, 83; biblical, 159; in preaching, 121, 124; religious, 63, 65, 68, 83, 97, 127, 159

Facilitating, 82, 84
Failure, homiletical, 159, 160
Faith, 41, 64, 69, 81, 92; of the preacher, 90, 91
Faithfulness, 49; of preacher, 42, 96
Fantasy, 41, 70
Farmer, H. H., 42
Faulkner, William, 53

Feedback, 105–6; group, 134
Feelings, 18, 41, 60, 64, 67, 73, 121, 127, 132, 161; denial of, 134; language of, 58
First-timeness, 148
Forgiveness, 83
Fosdick, Harry Emerson, 3, 20, 49, 125, 140, 146, 147
Frankl, Viktor, 9
Free association, 141
Freedom, 8, 9, 78, 99, 133
Frustration, 78, 83
Fry, John, 5
Future, 141

Geography, biblical, 32–34
Gerbner, George, 108
Gilkey, Langdon, 67, 73
Gnosticism, 20
God, presence of, 58, 95, 129, 131
Gospel, 13, 65, 133; power of, 60
Gossip, Arthur John, 150
Grace, 7, 19, 58, 63, 68, 73–75, 78, 83, 85, 92, 99, 122
Grief, 19, 38, 77, 134
Growth, church, 78; human, 22, 38, 90, 94, 95, 96; in faith, 42, 98; religious, 159
Guilt, 19, 133, 160

Happiness, 10, 85
Healing, 7–13, 78, 111, 133, 136, 146, 150
Health, 15
Hearing, 72, 98, 140
Helping skills, 80
Helplessness, 19, 38
Hermeneutical circle, 30, 125
Hermeneutics, 34, 96, 97, 124, 128
Hiltner, Seward, 15, 16, 43, 84
Hofstadter, Richard, 36
Homiletics, 31, 35, 45, 75, 80, 107, 113, 158, 159; teaching, 91, 112
Honesty, 22, 90, 102
Hope, 42, 75, 124, 131, 134
Humanness, 43, 73

Ideas, 51, 52; central, 131, 137; for sermons, 53, 92, 120, 125, 131; inventory of, 52–58, 120, 135–39
Illumination, 8–12

Illustrations, 3, 4, 20, 44, 45, 46, 60, 64
Images, in sermons, 137; in thinking, 52, 69; of ministry, 79, 80
Imagination, 22, 31, 40, 45, 104, 112, 141, 158
Immediacy, 36, 142
Incarnation, 7, 43
Individualization, 13, 106
Information, 3, 5, 19, 20, 37, 101, 107, 108, 111; processing, 30, 70
Insight, 31, 34, 141
Intellectualization, 18, 64, 106
Intensity, of experience, 74
Interpretation, 27, 28, 82, 84, 92, 126; in language, 63, 67, 83; of texts, 56; oral, 148, 154; theological, 63, 74, 123
Interpretative frame, 104
Interpretative potential, 27
Introduction, to sermon, 46, 96, 101–6, 160
Intuition, 116
Invitation, 2, 32, 93, 133
Involvement, of listeners, 36

Jargon, theological, 60, 72, 96, 131
Jesus, 44, 49, 67, 69, 72, 74, 77, 84, 89, 95, 99, 124, 126
Joy, 60, 122, 135
Judgment, 84; divine, 64
Justice, 111

Kardiner, Abram, 10
Kelley, Dean, 78–79
Kerygma, 159
Kingdom of God, 66, 128
Knowledge, 76
Koinonia, 106
Kopp, Sheldon, 21, 38

Language, 51, 103, 108, 117; and experience, 61–68; and reality, 60; connectedness of, 61–68; context for, 61, 69–75; descriptive, 63, 123; diagnostic, 82; interpretative, 63; misuse of, 59–68; oddity of, 65; of preaching, 60; of religious experience, 58, 161
Languages, of preaching, 58–75
Laypeople, 42, 105, 109, 144

Learning theory, 5
Lectionary, 55–58
Liberation, 89
Listeners, 62, 132, 155
Listening behavior, 23, 38, 103, 134
Literalism, biblical, 60, 67, 68
Liturgical calendar, 119
Loss, 134
Love, 14–17, 22, 30, 60, 63, 130,
    133; of God, 67, 69, 72, 124
Luther, Martin, 147
Lying, 145

Manipulation, 11, 113
Manuscript, for preaching, 150, 154
Marshall, Peter, 146
Mass media, 107, 108
Massa, Conrad, 56
Mather, Cotton, 147
Meaning, 28, 69, 79, 91; loss of, 8,
    78, 92
Memorizing sermons, 154
Message features, second-level, 20,
    108
Messages, 19, 20, 69, 89, 101, 103;
    form of, 158; meaning of, 69;
    transmission of, 28; unconscious
    41
Metacommunication, 28, 99–106
Metaphor, 65
Method, for preaching, 40, 115–34
Mind of Christ, 17, 86
Ministry, 76, 80, 86, 138; themes in,
    120
Mission, 37
Movement, text to sermon, 117
Muehl, William, 11
Mystery, 74, 136; of eucharist, 131;
    of language, 65

Narcissism, 17, 18, 21
Narrative, 4, 123, 149; realism,
    141
Needs, and God's action, 64; felt,
    61; preaching to, 39–44, 46, 55,
    159, 161
Neoorthodoxy, 128
Niemöller, Martin, 146
Noise, 121
Novak, Michael, 53
Nurture, 77, 95, 112

Objective, behavioral, 122; of
    teaching, 159
Objectivity, 55, 58, 120
Orchard, W. E., 158
Organization in sermons, 10, 60, 94
Outcomes of preaching, 17, 93, 103,
    117, 122, 123, 158
Outline, of sermon, 131
Overpreparation of sermons, 30–34

Pain, 22
Parable, 9, 77, 126
Paradox, 20
Parish ministry, 30
Participation, congregation's in
    preaching, 98–106, 155, 159
Pastor, role of, 40
Pastoral care, 20, 39, 76, 101
Pastoral visitation, 47
Pathology, religious, 18
Perception, 28, 121, 159
Personality, truth through, 90, 91
Persuasion, 108
Peter, 124
Piaget, Jean, 37, 61–62, 64
Piety, 75, 183
Pilgrimage, 41, 90, 103
Plagiarism, in preaching, 144–55
Planning of sermons, 53, 54, 58,
    116–34
Point of contact, 91, 127–29, 142
Power in preaching, 47, 48, 123
Prayer, 41
Preacher, person of, 90–93, 105–6,
    120
Preaching, conservative 78; event,
    106; of Jesus, 36; pastoral, 147;
    task of, 114, 155; topical, 125
Preparation of sermons, 30, 86,
    91–93, 95–97, 106, 115–34, 140,
    141, 159
Prepared conversation, 154
Presbyterians, 110, 111
Preunderstanding, 27, 55, 56, 125
Privatization, 13, 106
Process of preaching, 93
Proclamation, 42, 80, 95
Promise, 37, 75, 133
Prophecy, 76, 77
Proposition, of sermon, 117, 122,
    131, 135

Pseudoinnocence, 22
Psychiatry, 83
Psychodynamics, 81–83
Psychologization, 13
Psychopathology, 72
Psychosomatic illness, 19
Psychotherapy, 18, 38, 43, 67, 145
Publics, in communication, 106–14, 116, 134
Pulpit greats, 146
Purposes of preaching, 1, 2, 13, 36, 38, 60, 94, 96, 104, 120, 121–23, 134, 142

Ramsey, Ian, 65
Reality, 8, 11, 59; language and, 86
Receivers, 28, 69–75, 89, 90, 93, 100, 109, 112, 140
Records, of sermons, 117
Redemption, experience of, 72; story of, 69
Rejection, 159
Relationships, 15–17, 18, 134; eroded, 145; pastoral, 40, 91; to God, 60
Relevance, 44–49, 75, 132–33, 143, 159
Remembering sermons, 94–98
Repentance, 13, 14
Resistance, 46, 84, 90, 130
Responsibility, 21, 23, 78, 82, 84, 133–34
Resurrection, 77
Revelation, 95, 99, 129
Rhetoric, 95, 102, 116, 124, 143
Rich, Charlie, 9
Ricoeur, Paul, 65
Risk, 22, 84
Role-taking in communication, 65

Sacraments, 43, 119, 131
Salvation, drama of, 72, 99; knowledge of, 131
Scene-setting, 33–34
Scherer, Paul, 15, 46, 125, 126, 146, 147
Schizophrenia, 43, 59, 71–72
Scotford, John, 91
Self-esteem, 14
Self-criticism, 58, 120
Self-reflection, of preacher, 34, 56

Sermon crafting, 93, 121, 124
Sermon topics, 29
Sermons, first-person, 104–5; historic, 144–55; pastoral, 106; teaching, 99; three point, 102
Simon, Ulrich, 7, 12
Simplicity, 8, 36, 45
Simplification, 94; oversimplification, 60
Sin, 63, 83, 130, 144
Sinfulness, 14, 27, 84
Skill, communication, 64; helping, 80
Speech, 100, 148
Standpoints for reality, 53
Stendahl, Krister, 13
Stephenson, William, 107
Stewardship, 146
Story, 4, 35, 83, 93, 100; in communication, 69–75; of salvation, 99; preacher's own, 120; retelling, 62–63, 73; sacred, 141; sermon as, 123–24
Storyteller, 160
Strategy of preaching, 48, 117
Stress, 37
Struggle, of congregation, 159; of preacher, 41, 90, 158
Students, M. Div., 78, 80, 112, 122, 125, 149, 150; D. Min., 80–81, 85
Style, 8, 25, 60, 93, 99, 102, 113, 116, 124, 142, 143; of talking, 62; theological, 63
Subjectivity, 27
Sullivan, Harry Stack, 43
Support, 134
Symbols, 27, 37
Systems theory, 83

Tactics of preaching, 51
Teaching sermon, 99
Technique in preaching, 48
Texts (biblical), encounter with, 91; interpreting, 26, 27, 96, 124; meaning of, 127, 131; selecting, 55–58, 91; use of, 64, 97, 117
Thematization, 67, 74, 127
Themes, in ministry, 120; in sermons, 54, 57, 116, 124, 137, 160; of experience, 73
Theodicy, 22, 37

Theology, 77; American, 75; conservative, 78; language of, 63–68, 83; liberal, 78; pastoral, 79

Therapeia, 82

Thinking, categories of, 52–58; process of, 52; theological, 54, 149

Topic sentence, 122

Topics, of preaching, 135; selection of, 107

Tradition, 32, 127

Transcendence, 31, 36, 42, 67

Transformation, 26–27

Transgeneration, of meaning, 70

Translation, 29, 65, 67, 69, 70, 73, 130

Transmission of messages, 69

Trust, 18, 22

Turner, Victor, 27

Uncertainty, 5–7, 20, 41, 42, 83, 92, 93, 121

Unconscious, the, 20, 42, 47, 48, 57–58, 74, 108, 113, 116, 132, 142, 146

Underpreparation of sermons, 30–34

Values, 10, 47, 76, 79, 107–8, 120, 127, 132

Verbal realism, 66–68, 73, 74

Vocation, communication as, 100

Von Allmen, J. J., 106

Welsh, Clement, 1, 5

Will of God, 8, 22, 43, 64, 95

Word of God, 26, 27, 41, 42, 73, 95

Word study, 130

Work of God, 44

Worksheet, sermon, 117–34

Worship, 14, 42, 104, 105, 119, 160

Worry, 136

Wyckoff, D. Campbell, 56

251
NGI

61157